IRON JANE

Iron Jane

It's time for a lasting, loving
ceasefire in the battle
between the sexes.

Lee Ezell
and Lela Gilbert

Servant Publications
Ann Arbor, Michigan

Vine Books is an imprint of Servant Publications
especially designed to serve evangelical Christians.

Published by Servant Publications
P.O. Box 8617
Ann Arbor, Michigan 48107

Cover design by Multnomah Graphics & Printing
Cover illustration by James Douglas Adams
Text design by Diane Bareis

    95 96 97 98 10 9 8 7 6 5 4 3

Printed in the United States of America
ISBN 0-89283-882-5

Library of Congress Cataloging-in-Publication Data

Ezell, Lee.
    Iron Jane : it's time for a lasting, loving ceasefire in the
battle of the sexes / Lee Ezell and Lela Gilbert.
        p.   cm.
    ISBN 0-89283-882-5 : $8.99 (est.)
    1. Sex role.   2. Gender identity.   3. Man-woman rela-
tionships.   I. Gilbert, Lela.   II. Title.
HQ1090.E94   1994
305.3--dc20   94-15474
                                                        CIP

Contents

Other Books by Lee Ezell

The Cinderella Syndrome
The Missing Piece
Pills for Parents in Pain

*Being powerful is like being a lady:
if you have to tell you are, you aren't!*

**Margaret Thatcher,
former British Prime Minister,
affectionately known as *The Iron Lady***

Chapter 1

Who Is Iron Jane?

Have you ever heard the legend of Iron John?

Iron John is featured in an ancient fairy tale, which Robert Bly, men's activist, author and poet, has used as the theme of a book bearing the same name. His writing provides a robust perspective on the modern man's search for male identity in a rapidly changing world.

Bly's book is a captivating and at times bewildering look at mythology, psychology, and sexuality, and many of the author's carefully conceived theories are not to be taken lightly by either men or women.

On a practical note, if you did run into Iron John, you probably wouldn't want to be caught dead with him. According to the legend, he's been living at the bottom of a pond for centuries, and he hasn't shaved for even longer. Antiperspirant could hardly help.

Some observers believe that the so-called "male movement," epitomized by *Iron John*, is a backlash response to the women's movement which began to impact society in the 1970s. They are convinced that men are simply trying to elbow their way back into power. Others would disagree, claiming that men lost their way a long time before the 1970s.

Is the male movement a war cry by men, demanding that some unwritten macho bill of rights be reinstated? Is a corresponding figure–Iron Jane–about to emerge? Is she a warrior too, her armor blazing in the sun, defensively prepared to confront the male power figure unleashed by Bly and his disciples?

> **The 90s Career Woman:**
> *Looks like a lady,*
> *acts like a man,*
> *works like a dog.*

Who is Iron Jane? A feminist may answer that Iron Jane is a character who is hard, aggressive, and thick-skinned. This individual is willing to take on any man, toe-to-toe, insult-for-insult. In the process she makes no apologies. This Iron Jane assumes that she has been victimized by males. Men are, in her view, the enemy. She has been hurt, and she must now defend herself from further injury.

But my Iron Jane is altogether different. She is not a warrior in a clanking suit of armor. She is a woman of soft heart, gentle face, and willing hands. The steel is in her soul. She isn't roaring with frustration at the men in her life, nor is she trying to become a man.

Instead she is curious about the undeniable differences between men and women. She wants to build bridges, not burn them. And she has dedicated her formidable, iron will to making the male-female interaction work the way God intended it to–body, soul, and spirit. Instead of a male-basher, she's a male-mesher.

Maybe another way to look at her is as a real "Steel Magnolia." The outside is delicate and sensitive. The inner woman is courageous, strong, and enduring. That strength can only come from spiritual depth and maturity. It isn't that she hasn't been hurt. She has. But she's chosen to forgive, heal, and move forward into the future with a positive attitude.

Women, like their male counterparts, are still trying to find their way toward peace and contentment in an uncertain world that is forever changing its rules. Fortunately, for those who want them, there are fixed standards still in place–guidelines about love, understanding, sacrifice, and compassion.

Bear in mind, however, that sometimes my Iron Jane is unable to resist the temptation to poke fun at the men in her life. Fortunately, she's not afraid to laugh at herself, either. If the pages that follow make you laugh, all the better. With any luck, we'll solve a few mysteries, kill off some stereo-types, avoid some crises, and open up some new channels of communication.

As for me, I'm hard to label. I'm not a traditional "feminist," although I applaud women being more involved in leadership and positions of influence. And though I'm a "traditional family values" person, I believe freedom should be offered equally to men and women.

Some cars sport a "Save the Whales" bumper sticker. I'd like to have one that says, *"Save the Males."* We can't permit masculinity to be obscured any more than femininity should be allowed to fade away.

ARE WOMEN THE WEAKER SEX?

The "weaker sex" may describe a lower average physical strength than males can develop. It may have to do with emotional fluctuations.

"Weaker" certainly isn't my preferred word to describe women, but in some ways "wounded" is. In the battle of the sexes, many women have been cut down in the prime of their lives. They've been broken and disabled, and they aren't prone to volunteer for the front lines again. When it comes to male-female tours of duty, they are the draft dodgers. Are they right to avoid the whole scene?

Maybe the bumper sticker is right: *LIFE IS HARD… THEN YOU DIE.* All of life involves struggle. But we have choices to make. We can spend our lives avoiding difficulties, stand as spectators on the sidelines, or jump in and take our chances.

Many women, particularly those who are deeply wounded, are afraid to take further risks. The fear of being hurt again increases when wounds have already been inflicted by men. Men seem to be a different breed… a different species.

Accepting and understanding the differences between men and women can *fortify* us against being injured by men, without lashing out in retaliation for the past.

In the process we create an Iron Jane.

I can recall one of the first times I stood up for myself with an intimidating man who was trying to take advantage of me. During a disagreement at work, I decided not to sound "retreat." Once my statement was made, the man glared at me in rage and said facetiously, "My, you are a *strong* woman!"

"Thank you!" I responded, much to his surprise. He thought he was insulting me, but I was pleased with his response.

I think strength is a plus in any woman. I appreciate a woman who is strong and courageous, whether or not I agree with her. And I know this: if her strength is under control, she can have successful relationships–even with men who feel threatened at first. She can be an Iron Jane.

> *We don't have to become angry women with hard, protective shells.*

What does Iron Jane look like? For one thing, she doesn't come noisily clanking into the room; her armor doesn't make her a loud, pushy broad. In order to be strong, we don't have to also become hostile women with hard, protective shells. You know those types when you meet them–they've been hurt in one relationship with a man, and that's the end of it: been there, done that, no thanks. There is a hardness about them. This kind of woman has built an impenetrable fortress around herself which no man dares approach.

Not Iron Jane. She has *inner toughness, but outer softness*. She is willing to risk again, having been fortified with enlightenment and forgiveness. She is not afraid to try again. She may be single, she may be married. She's determined not to surrender, not to overwhelm, not to emasculate but to coexist peacefully and joyfully with the males in her life.

WOMEN AREN'T THE ONLY WALKING WOUNDED

All that may sound to you like a one-sided scenario. A woman gets hurt. She withdraws. The man is unconcerned, and blithely goes on from there to hurt another woman. That is hardly the case. Men are wounded too; some of them deeply damaged by the selfishness of women. My heart goes out to the modern male who honestly wishes to understand his role better. The reason books like *Iron John* were written in the first place was because modern men feel they've lost something important. They feel diminished, not only in matters of power but in spirit and in soul. They may see the history books full of male heroes who are fearless in their conquests, but the females who present them, such as moms and teachers, give a mixed message: typical boyish behavior is wrong. Be careful, don't roughhouse, don't shout, don't get dirty, and so forth. In short, emulate the role-models, but be more like a girl. So males are confused and feel they can't win. In case you think this is nonsense, take a moment to consider the following.

14

HERE'S HOW LIFE LOOKS TO THE MAN OF THE 90s:

◆ When a woman has a boring job with low pay, that's exploitation. When a man has a boring job with low pay, he should get off his duff and find something better.

◆ When a man stays home to do the housework, he's a wimp. When a man goes out and works long hours, he has abandoned his family.

◆ When a woman gets promoted ahead of a man, that's equal opportunity. When a man gets promoted ahead of a woman, that is sexual discrimination.

◆ When a man tells a woman she looks great, it's sexual harassment. When a man doesn't tell a woman she looks great, he's demonstrating male indifference.

◆ When a man tries to keep himself in shape, that's macho male ego. When a man doesn't, he's a slob.

◆ When a man makes a decision without consulting his woman, he's an arrogant sexist. When a woman makes a decision without consulting her man, she's a liberated woman.

◆ When a man asks a woman to do something unpleasant, it's called domination. When a woman asks a man to do something unpleasant, it's called doing her a favor.

◆ When a man is proud of his achievements, he's egotistical. When a woman is proud of hers, it's a victory for women in a male-dominated world. (If she has no achievements, it is evidence of male oppression.)

◆ When a man wants affection, he's accused of selfishly thinking of nothing but sex. When a man is too tired to make love, he's accused of selfishly withholding sex.

◆ When a man expresses the differences between males and females, it's sexism. When a woman expresses the same differences, it's a brave statement on behalf of affirmative action.

This rather ruthless list communicates a very important aspect of the Iron Jane/Iron John dilemma: there are two sides to it!

AVOIDING STEREOTYPES

In the pages that follow, we're going to examine some popular ideas about men and women as well as some statements by experts who have made a career of tallying up the differences. But let's begin by saying that there are exceptions to every rule.

There is something in me that resents being pigeonholed, slotted into one category or another. For example, "man is fact-oriented; woman is feeling-oriented" can be interpreted to say that men are the only logical beings on planet Earth, while all women are emotional airheads. It can also mean that each sex has wonderful gifts to offer the other. Truth can be twisted; generalizations can diminish truth.

Besides, the stereotypes don't always apply. For instance, men are notoriously depicted as people who hate shopping. Lots of women-at-the-mall jokes are told, usually by men. But in my marriage, those roles are reversed. Hal is a world-class shopper; I hate shopping. He can't wait for the day-after-Thanksgiving sales so he can meet the challenge of overcrowded parking lots and cash register lines. For me, the whole process is insanity.

Hal and I don't act this way because we are acting out some predetermined male-female roles. We act this way because crowded shops make me nervous, while my husband has a phlegmatic personality and never gets ruffled.

> *Some men never have stress;
> they're carriers.*

PERSONALITY, NOT GENDER

Much of our behavior stems from temperament, which predisposes us to a certain pattern of behavior. For instance, one personality type tends to be work-oriented, high-achieving and extroverted. Another will be more introspec-tive, analytically creative, and introverted.

Whether we are men or women, we are born with certain

characteristics. That doesn't mean we are forever locked into our own natural weaknesses, but it does mean that we cannot escape the dictates of our natural temperament.

I speak all over the world, and I often ask a question of my audience: "How many of you are married to someone who is the *total opposite* of you?" As hands are raised, a murmur ripples through the crowd. I watch their surprise and fascination. They are amazed to discover what an overwhelmingly high percentage of couples are total opposites. They must have forgotten Burns and Allen, Ricky and Lucy and a host of others.

Dr. Robert Schuller, pastor of California's Crystal Cathedral put it this way, "My wife and I are different; I'm more prone to be *schematic,* while she is *pragmatic.* When I told her years ago that I had an idea for a 'Crystal Cathedral,' her response was something like this: "How are we going to clean the windows?"

NO ABSOLUTES NEED APPLY

Let's bear in mind that some differences are based on gender, some on personality and some on other assorted idiosyncrasies. Let's avoid generalizing, and yet see the patterns that tend to repeat themselves in our male–female relations.

Most of all, let's lay down our lethal weapons and make up our minds to laugh at ourselves as well as at our significant others (who also deserve being laughed at now and then!). After all, if we can't laugh at ourselves, I figure that a lot of other folks will be more than happy to do it for us!

Let's take a closer look at just what makes men and women so very different and at times so seemingly incompatible. Perhaps through heightened awareness, and a commitment to unity, we can establish a demilitarized zone in the raging "battle of the sexes."

Don't think of it as victory, and don't feel you've surrendered, either. Just see, in the pages that follow, the opportunity to sign a treaty for lasting peace between us women and those ever present men that we can't live with, and we can't live without.

> *Relationships are a lot*
> *like the Army:*
> *Everyone complains, but*
> *most re-enlist!*

Chapter 2

We're Wired So Differently!

Judy is in the very final stages of labor. She is push, push, pushing to deliver her first child. The process is nearly over.

Her husband Terry's face is almost as sweaty as hers. His eyes are troubled and worried. He wants the ordeal to be over, and for his beloved wife to be completely out of pain and danger. And she senses his love and compassion. In spite of everything else, his hand feels good in hers.

Suddenly the agony is over. The doctor scoops up the

still-wet baby, and holds it up for all to see.

"Congratulations–it's a boy!"

Terry beams, prouder than words can express. Judy, weary as she is, glances at her husband and nods in approval. "You've got a son, Terry," she whispers softly.

He kisses her cheek.

It's interesting to note that, in this tender moment, nobody looks at the doctor with narrowed, suspicious eyes and says, "What do you mean, 'it's a boy'?"

No brand-new parent glares at the hard-working medical team in the maternity section of the hospital and growls, "How can you say 'It's a boy'? You don't know what you're talking about! You're going to have to prove it to me!"

No skeptical new father confronts the Ob-Gyn and asks for proof. "A boy, huh? That's what you think. So what makes you so sure?"

BOUNCING BOYS; ADORABLE GIRLS

It doesn't take a rocket scientist to understand the most obvious difference between baby girls and baby boys. We all come into the world naked and clearly defined in our gender. No questions, no debates.

Following that first declaration in the delivery room, it doesn't take family and friends long to start saying things like, "He's all boy, isn't he?" Dressed in a miniature L.A. Rams football jersey, the little guy gets tossed, bounced, and wrestled about with great enthusiasm.

Meanwhile, in the pale pink nursery, both men and women tend to hold infant girls as if they were fragile porcelain. Little "princesses" are soon clothed in flowers and lace; rose-colored dresses hang in tiny closets. And dolls, not Matchbox cars and soccer balls, begin to fill the toy chest.

Yes, folks. There's a difference. A big difference. And the older the baby boy and the baby girl get, the more evident the differences will become. Unfortunately, it won't be long before male and female idiosyncrasies can cause hurts. Fathers will misunderstand daughters; mothers won't grasp the sensitivities of their sons. Hurts may beget anger. Anger may beget bitterness and self-protection. Opposing territories will be quickly staked out and jealously guarded.

IRRECONCILABLE DIFFERENCES?

"He's a typical little boy, isn't he?" is eventually re-worded: "Unbelievable! Isn't that just like a *man?*"

"You're Daddy's precious girl" becomes, "Stop your complaining! You sound just like your mother."

Time passes, and boys and girls enter the hormone zone. They become teenagers. He says about his sweet dream girl, "She's so confusing. First, she acts like she likes me, then she won't talk to me. I don't understand her at all."

She says, "Why doesn't he call me? If he really liked me, he'd call me. He's warm one minute and cold the next. I don't get it." Voila–another Jane and John have marched from toyland to conflict, and the battle of the sexes has been passed on to yet another generation. Both will need some protective armor.

There's no doubt about the outward, visible differences between the sexes. If you don't think those differences cause problems, consider the woman in Virginia who recently emasculated her husband in a rage. She took the most radical step imaginable to try to remedy a prevalent type of marital conflict. Ever since her brutal indiscretion, it is said that more men sleep on their stomachs in Virginia than anywhere else in the world....

Besides wars over sexual conduct, there are also raging battles fought every day over toilet seats that are left in the upright position. The toilet seat confrontations may even be more dangerous than the squeeze-the-toothpaste-tube-from-the-bottom wars or the dirty-socks-and-underwear-all-over-the-place skirmishes. We laugh about stereotypical conflicts, but the truth is...

SEXUAL DIFFERENCES ARE MORE THAN SKIN DEEP

Different to the core. Quite apart from reproductive distinctions, boys and girls, men and women are dissimilar in countless other ways. Those differences are clearly observable down to the very cells. For example, as a result of chromosome patterns, the chemical structure of a man's body differs from that of a woman. Bone structures in men and women are not the same; women's heads are shorter, as are their legs. Their hips are broader than a man's (to their eternal dismay) and many of their internal organs are larger.

Counter to the claims of many feminists, men are 50 percent physically stronger than women. So why did we make them stop opening doors and carrying packages for us? (Maybe that's what keeps Jane Fonda working out. She has to keep her strength up, so she can carry her part of the unisex load.)

It's interesting to note: most psychologists agree that women are emotionally stronger than men. We'll deal with emotional differences in another chapter. But the man's physical strength is obviously intended to serve the purpose of providing for and protecting his family, while the woman's emotional strength is essential to mothering and, yes, nurturing a healthy, fruitful marital relationship with... a man.

> ### *I don't Suffer from PMS, I have UMS:* Ugly Mood Swings

Of course male and female glands put out different hormones. Women have a complex hormonal cycle which affects both sexuality and moods. Men sometimes complain about this cycle. However, if you ask most women, they would say that men only have one hormone–testosterone. And women usually agree that, in the realm of male hormones, that is quite enough.

Heaven knows, it gets the job done.

A woman's cycle, including that mysterious malady known as PMS, is the subject of many jokes, much speculation and a certain quiet reverence in the minds of many males. Men are both intrigued and intimidated by women's invisible, clock-like regularity; they can change from The Total Woman into The Total Witch from Hades every month. Women don't really understand it themselves. (However, my husband Hal says he doesn't mind when I have PMS. He has his ESPN.)

Metabolism and blood. Besides their definitive reproductive characteristics, a woman's basal metabolism is normally lower than a man's, which means she can't eat as many hot fudge sundaes as he can without wearing them on her thighs. At the same time, she can better tolerate temperature extremes. (In other words, she's resistant to Celsius but more vulnerable to cellulite.)

Sad to say, men have their corresponding physical impairments. It may be that when God took out Adam's rib to make woman that he let things slide into an area right around the belt line–where beer bellies begin.

Speaking of cells, a female's blood has 20 percent fewer red cells, which may or may not shed light on the repentant husband's plea, "Don't be so judgmental! What did you expect? I'm just a red-blooded American guy." Just being "a guy" may not be enough of an excuse for sexual improprieties, but it does explain some distinctive behavior.

"Brainwashed" even before we're born. Medical experts claim that while a fetus is gestating, a sort of chemical bath takes place inside the embryonic sac, which causes boy and girl babies to function differently after birth. (When explaining this to your man, try to avoid saying, "Say, I understand you guys are brainwashed...")

For one thing, this bath causes females to be more in tune with the right side of the brain. And what does the right brain do? It creates feelings and communication skills. It inspires creativity and intuition (yes, women are often more intuitive). It is more loving than logical.

Women have more rapid heartbeats–eighty beats per minute compared with seventy-two for men. Could this be true because thinking about relationships is more exciting than reading *How to Fix Your Car's Engine?* Or is it because women drink more coffee because they've been up all night with fussy babies?

No matter–they live longer than men, but that's good news/bad news, too. By the time a woman reaches the end of her life, all the good potential relationships are gone and she has nothing left to think about. Chances are, when you see me reading *How to Fix Your Car's Engine,* you can safely assume that the end really is near. (By the way, if you're a female auto mechanic, don't be offended–I wish I shared your ability!)

Males have experienced their own unique chemical bath, and are therefore inclined to utilize the left brain more comfortably. To the left side of the brain, facts are more significant than feelings; logic supersedes hunches; competitiveness outdistances intimacy. Males are less relationship-oriented than females, and yet they long, almost despairingly, for the relationships and emotional intimacy they sometimes can't seem to put together.

GLOBAL VS. LOBAL

We could say that girls tend to be more "global" in their thought processes. That *is* a technical way of saying that they use both brain lobes more efficiently than boys. That *is not* a technical way of saying that women are smarter. It probably does mean that men are more compartmentalized in their thinking than women.

All too often this physiological thinking pattern causes men to truly have *one track minds.* So while a woman can very easily talk on the phone, work in the kitchen and watch TV all at the same time, her man can only focus on one thing to the exclusion of everything else around him. That's why it's not wise to try to communicate on his Track Two while he's tuned into Track One.

We'll talk about communication more thoroughly in a later chapter but for now, consider this suggestion:

> ***Wait till you have a man's attention before you try to communicate with him.***

A CASE OF FEMALE INTUITION

As we noted, it's probably the left brain/right brain difference that causes intuitive women to "have a hunch" about something, and not be able to explain it. It happens like this:

• "Wait 'til you hear about the great deal I fell into today!" Paul reported excitedly. "Remember the guy we met Friday night? His name was Louie?"

Tonya, Paul's girlfriend listened intently. "You mean the big guy with the beeper and the cellular phone? He was quite a charmer."

Paul nodded, a vague uncertainty clouding his face. He hadn't remembered much about Louie except that he drove away from the party in a late model BMW with a statuesque brunette on his arm.

"Yeah, I guess that was him. Anyway... " he slapped down a pile of brochures, "he has this real estate investment deal that offers terrific short-term turnaround. I told him I'd love to get in on it. He said, 'Great! Just have a check for me by Friday. I promise you a quick, sure profit.'"

Immediately Tonya's early warning system went off inside. She tried to choose her words carefully. "Are you asking me what I think, or telling me you're going to invest in this, no matter what?"

Paul paused. He hadn't anticipated any reaction from Tonya, one way or the other. "Well, of course I want your opinion about it."

Tonya shook her head, a troubled look in her eyes. "I

wish I could explain, but I just don't have a good feeling about it. There's something about that guy I don't trust."

"Oh, so it's your 'female intuition' trip again?"

Paul was annoyed. He smirked sarcastically as he rifled through the brochures, trying to find a chart. "Just look at this! Look at these figures!"

Tonya nodded. There was no way to argue with the numbers Paul was holding up in front of her. She sighed, "I know. But the figures don't mean as much to me as the way that guy comes off. There's something wrong with him. Why don't you give yourself a little time?"

Even though initially he was angry with Tonya, Paul chose to humor her. He told Louie that he couldn't come up with the money before the first of the month. By that time, somehow big Louie was hard to reach, and before long Paul learned that he'd left town. Something about embezzlement…

Now that story doesn't mean that women are always right and men are always wrong. But it does demonstrate a peculiar tendency that some women have to "just know" something. When they do, they are sometimes unable to give a logical explanation for their feelings.

JUMPING TO CONCLUSIONS–INTUITIVELY

We could also turn it around another way. Sometimes a woman gets "a feeling," followed by another and another. Before long, she's come to an obvious conclusion–

obviously wrong, once her male counterpart presents the facts.

> **Female intuition is valuable, but not infallible.**

Margo had this strange feeling that her husband Bill wasn't as much in love with her as he used to be. For almost two weeks, he had come home, eaten his dinner in near-silence, turned on the television for the evening and then gone to bed with hardly a word. He was pre-occupied morning, noon, and night. Although he'd been eager to make love, he hadn't really "been there" emotionally.

Margo was reading a romance novel in which one of the male characters was having an affair with a woman. In the book's story development, the man's behavior seemed all too much like Bill's. Could the novel be God's way of warning her about something? Margo's fears deepened with every passing day. She decided to talk to her friend Kathleen.

Unfortunately, Kathleen's first marriage had ended because her husband had been emotionally unavailable. He had been cold, detached, and disinterested. Kathleen had never gotten over the rejection.

"I've been there, Margo. Believe me. And in my opinion, men are all alike. You know–they just aren't able to love the way we do, and if you've seen one, you've seen them all. Bill's exactly like Carl was, and forgive me for saying so, but I think you've got some rough days ahead."

Margo's sinking feeling continued to deepen. She became obsessed with the problem, and the more she thought about it, the worse it got. Finally, driving home from the market, she clicked on the radio just in time to hear the Righteous Brothers singing "You've Lost that Loving Feeling."

She burst into tears, stormed into the house past Bill, and locked herself in their room, sobbing uncontrollably.

Bill pounded on the bedroom door until she let him in.

"How could you do this to me?" she demanded. His face was completely blank. What on earth was Margo talking about? Fortunately, Bill had the grace to hold his trembling wife in his arms while he probed for answers. Gradually the story spilled out, in bits and pieces.

Bill was completely taken by surprise. He hadn't even been aware that his behavior had changed. He explained that he'd been having a problem at work, for which he partly blamed himself. He hadn't wanted to talk about it, because he felt somewhat ashamed that he wasn't handling it better. He'd also had an uncomfortable conversation with his father a week before. And to make matters worse, he had been fighting off a sore throat for several days. Bill was very logical—so logical that, at first, Margo didn't believe him.

"Are you sure you aren't having an affair?" she sniffled.

"An affair? With whom? You've got to be kidding! Is that what you thought? Good grief!"

Bill's rather loud burst of laughter convinced her that her "hunches" were off base. Margo's reactions were intuitive, although inaccurately so. Bill's were logical–he was trying to relieve his stress by removing himself from his problems once he got home from work.

The confusion came because he had left Margo out by not discussing his problem with her. She knew something was wrong, and she assumed the worst.

GATHERERS AND HUNTERS

Male-female differences don't stop with facts vs. feelings. Stories are often told about the way men and women function differently at the shopping mall or the market. As a result of their cavewoman heritage, women are supposed to be "gatherers," prowling from store to store, collecting necessities for the family. They spend hours seeking the best supplies for home and hearth, satisfying a sort of "nesting" urge.

It's been said that women like clothes while men prefer cars. I myself like cars (because they take me to places where I can buy clothes!).

Men, the true hunters, head directly for the desired product. Like expert swordsmen, they draw their American Express cards out of their leather wallets, and conquer the sale. Proudly they return to the car, prey in hand. (Usually no one is there to greet them–the wives are in Nordstrom's, seeking Liz Claiborne necessities to gather.)

Men cannot relate to our need for a wide selection of clothing–that's one reason most men hate shopping. Because this is widely known, every department store designs its Men's Department on the first floor, twenty feet from the entrance. That's about as far as a man cares to venture in.

A lot of guys could put on a uniform every morning and be perfectly happy. Meanwhile, many women get satisfaction out of the daily choosing of a different outfit depending on what (or whom) the day holds, and how she feels. She may even change outfits a few times that day depending on her mood.

You'll never hear a man complain "Oh, no! That man over there has on the same blue suit as I do." Actually, I suspect men are quite happy if they all happen to look alike; that reassures them that they haven't made a mistake!

Of course, it's not at all fair to generalize. There are women who insist that their men have garage–and closet-"gathering" tendencies. And one wife I know cannot comprehend why, when she sends her husband to the market for toilet paper, he comes home with light bulbs, ice cream and dog food, but no toilet paper. Perhaps the prey wasn't appealing to him. Even the most able hunters sometimes need lists.

DIFFERENT DOESN'T MEAN WRONG!

So are guys designed differently from us? You bet they are! But if we accept this as a *challenge to mesh* rather than

We're Wired So Differently!

as some hidden male agenda for driving us crazy, we'll strap on our "Understanding and Accepting" armor, and walk back onto the battlefield.

A hair stylist at my beauty shop once said, "Relationships are impossible. Men are out to get what they can–without commitment. All men are blundering idiots without a sensitive bone in their bodies."

I smiled and said, "Well some of them commit, otherwise none of us would be married."

She shook her head, looking at me as if I'd lost my last marble. "Yeah, sure. But after they marry you, they change. None of them can be faithful. They don't think faithfulness matters. And another thing…"

On and on she went. This is the kind of thinking that fans the feminist fires and adds to the number of bitter women who only look to other women for intimacy. Iron Jane has to fight her way clear of anti-man prejudices, strengthened by her awareness that some differences are simply physiological.

We'll discover in other chapters that there are qualities in men and women that seem to parallel the differences in their physical bodies.

> *A woman naturally embraces and enfolds people in relationships.*
> *A man tends to stand on his own, valuing independence and singularity.*

35

An interesting possibility is that our human bodies are simply visible representations of our inner selves, and that our sexual characteristics originate in our hearts and souls.

Psychologist Dr. Larry Crabb discusses that thought-provoking possibility in his book *Men and Women; Enjoying the Difference:*

> The idea that our distinctively designed bodies reflect distinctively shaped souls triggers more questions...
>
> Is there something uniquely feminine about a woman that makes it more natural for her to *receive* her husband in their everyday relationship, the way she physically receives him in the bedroom? Is there something uniquely masculine about a man that makes it more natural for him to *move toward* his wife in their relationship the way he physically moves toward her in the bedroom?[1]

Clearly, God created differences between man and woman, from the most minute amounts of DNA to the distinct design of the male and female form. Perhaps that is only the beginning. Maybe the differences that we struggle with are God-given, purposeful, and reaching into the very core of our beings–emotionally, intellectually, socially, and perhaps even spiritually.

If we were intended to be different but complementary, then let's make an all-out effort to discover the ways in which we are uniquely fitted together like a hand in a glove. That kind of information could revolutionize our relationships. It could transform our emotional interaction. Who knows? Loving and being loved might just turn out to be more rewarding than we ever imagined possible.

> *Put on the armor of Understanding and Acceptance; men and women are wired differently.*

Chapter 3

Two Different Worlds

Hal and I were packing materials into our trunk after teaching a class on communication. He seemed rather subdued, and I asked him why. "Is something wrong, Hal?"

"No, everything's just great… 'Gracie.'"

"Gracie? As in Burns and Allen Gracie?"

We got into the car and there was a gap in the conversation while he started the engine. "Yeah," he continued, "I don't like playing the straight man every time. I set you up and you tell all the jokes."

I was surprised by his complaint, but quickly offered a solution. "Well, would you like to tell some jokes next week?"

He glanced at me as he checked the rear view mirror. "Yeah. Why should you get all the laughs?"

We worked out a few jokes, and the next week he did his thing. The jokes bombed–he either got lost in the middle or forgot the punch line. Afterwards, while we were packing up again, I heard him mumble. "I guess it's not so bad."

"What's not so bad?"

"Being George Burns. It's more like me, and it seems more natural for you to clown around. You can have the jokes from now on, Gracie. George lived longer anyway…"

When it comes to socializing, men and women are from two different worlds. Hal and I have never had any trouble seeing this, not only because we're man and woman, but because of our very different personalities. As you can see from what happened, it's easier for me to connect with an audience on an emotional level than it is for Hal. In some ways, making emotional connections is easier for many other women, too. But why? How do these differences begin? The following story may provide a clue or two.

BABY DOLLS VS. SOCCER BALLS

In sheer delight, six-year-old Cindy opened her Christmas presents, one after another. She pulled each new gift out of its gleaming wrappings. With anticipation and joy she embraced a lifelike newborn doll. Along with it came a set of baby bottles, miniature clothing, diapers, blankets, and even a toy pacifier.

Once Christmas dinner was over, Cindy gathered up her new playthings and rushed across the street to visit her best friend Ashley. Ashley had received a beautiful new Barbie doll, which was accompanied by a wardrobe of gowns, bathing suits, business attire, and all the right accessories. Within minutes, the two little girls were quietly playing in Ashley's room. Cindy was caring for her newborn and Ashley was dressing Barbie.

As the girls talked back and forth, Ashley remarked, "Look, isn't this a pretty dress? Barbie looks beautiful in it."

Cindy nodded, rocking her baby contentedly. "She *is* beautiful. When my baby grows up, she'll look just like Barbie. Hey! Let's pretend my doll is Barbie when she was a baby..."

Ashley nodded excitedly. "Or we can pretend that she's Barbie's baby..."

The girls played together for hours, each enjoying her Christmas gifts, sharing ideas and sometimes switching roles–Ashley took care of the baby while Cindy dressed Barbie for a special night on the town. Although the girls could hear the sound of boys playing outside, they paid little attention to the raucous noise.

The scene in the street bore little resemblance to the girls' tranquil playtime. Ashley's eight-year-old brother Cory had received a new soccer ball for Christmas. He had recruited several neighborhood boys into a game of kick-back which had eventually turned into an argumentative, unofficiated free-for-all.

Shawn, the biggest boy on the street, had arrived soon after Cory and his friends began to play. Because of his size and his athletic ability, he organized the game to his advantage. Cory and Steve, two boys closest to Shawn in size and age, were assigned to oppose him. Shawn teamed himself with a five-year-old, who felt very fortunate to be playing with the big kids.

Once Cory and Steve scored twice against Shawn and his miniature teammate, Shawn quickly reorganized the game so that he would win. He teamed himself with Cory, and the two of them promptly overpowered Steve and the hapless five-year-old.

After Steve complained about the unfairness of the teams, Shawn dumped Cory and recruited Steve. Steve felt honored to play with Shawn, and the two of them completely overwhelmed Cory and the five-year-old.

Cory was furious. "It's my ball! I get to pick the teams."

And so it went. During the same period of time that Ashley and Cindy were engaged in quiet, noncompetitive play, the neighborhood boys were carrying on a wild exercise in competition and conflict. And what happens when children grow up? Women usually connect with each other effortlessly; men feel most connected with other men through military, sports, and college activities.

ASSOCIATION OR AUTONOMY?

Deborah Tannen, Ph.D., in her book *You Just Don't Understand*, says,

... worlds of play shed light on the world views of women and men in relationships. The boy's play illuminates why men would be on the lookout for signs they are being put down or told what to do. The chief commodity that is bartered in the boy's hierarchical world is *status*, and their way to achieve and maintain status is to give orders and get others to follow them....

These dynamics are not the ones that drive girls' play. The chief commodity that is bartered in the girl's community is *intimacy*.[1]

In the early years of childhood, two chief social concerns emerge that will set the genders apart for the rest of their lives. For males, it's *independence*. For females, it's *intimacy*.

Is the root of those differences cultural? Is it the result of some deeply embedded genetic programming? In either case, it ultimately becomes a social difference: men *treasure their autonomy*; women *yearn for close association*. And, as we know, the two points of view don't mix too well.

> *Men value independence just as deeply as women value intimacy.*

WHY DOES HE ALWAYS PULL AWAY?

Now it's not too hard to pick up these clashing social inclinations in daily life. Most women have noticed a particular tendency in men. Let me give you an idea of how it works.

Jan and Terry have been dating for a year, and they are talking tentatively about getting married. They *would* be getting married if it weren't for Jan's mistrust of her boyfriend. It isn't that Terry has ever cheated on Jan. He hasn't. But he always seems to be pushing her away, then drawing her close, then pushing her away again. She secretly suspects that he has some kind of deep-seated emotional problems.

On Terry's birthday, for example, Jan prepared a beautiful dinner for him. She prepared all his favorite foods, borrowed her mother's best china and silver, lit candles, and treated him like a king.

And her efforts were not unrewarded. As they ate, and later as they sat beside a crackling fire listening to love songs, Terry began to bare his soul to Jan.

He told her about his parent's divorce, and when he talked about it, to the surprise of both of them, he teared up and began to cry. Jan comforted him. She held him closer. The evening was more warm and intimate than anything either of them had experienced before. It felt to both of them like a turning point in their relationship.

And it was sincere, Jan thought afterward. *It wasn't just some stupid fantasy. We were being real with each other!*

But... for the days that followed, Jan's thoughts were full of rage. She fully expected Terry to call her the next day, which was Sunday, to affirm her, and to continue the soft, gentle mood of the evening before.

The phone never rang Sunday.

It didn't ring Monday, either.

Or Tuesday.

Jan was so angry and frustrated that she nearly called Terry and told him not to bother calling her again. Terry called Wednesday sounding desperate. He reported to Jan that there had been a family crisis. Jan rushed to the hospital to be at his side while his mother underwent emergency surgery.

Once the crisis had passed, Jan couldn't resist a strategic question. "Have you been mad at me?" she asked Terry, fully expecting the worst.

"Mad?" Terry's face was completely blank. "Why would I be mad? What made you think that?"

"I haven't heard from you since Saturday. I thought you'd call."

Terry looked at Jan as if *her* sanity were in question. "Just because I don't call you doesn't mean I'm mad. Besides, you could have called *me!*"

THE SNAP OF THE ELASTIC

Terry and Jan are not at all unusual. Our own experience bears it out: men can be fascinated with Outer Space but disinterested in exploring Inner Space. Women may be more interested in Inner Space, but we still need help understanding how we really tick.

As Dr. John Gray says in his book *Men Are from Mars, Women Are from Venus:*

Men begin to feel their need for autonomy and independence *after* they have fulfilled their need for intimacy

Automatically when he begins to pull away, she begins to panic. What she doesn't realize is that when he pulls away and fulfills his need for autonomy then suddenly he will want to be intimate again. A man automatically alternates between needing intimacy and autonomy.[2]

That quote is from a chapter Dr. Gray has aptly entitled, "Men Are Like Rubber Bands." Another chapter might well have been called, "Women Ought to Learn to Snap Them Back into Shape!" The fact is, we get a bit frustrated dealing with that stretched-out elastic.

We either react to a man's need for independence by feeling utterly rejected, or we decide to reform him. (When I walked to the altar with Hal, I thought "... I'll *alter* him!") Neither approach is particularly constructive to our relationships. Why?

Because men value independence just as deeply as women value intimacy.

One troublesome aspect to the rubber band syndrome is that when men do snap back into place, their women misconstrue the situation. They think the whole relationship has to be rebuilt from the ground up. Once the man calls, having emerged from his silence, he acts as if nothing has happened. He does this for one simple reason: as far as he's concerned, nothing *has* happened.

Meanwhile, his lady thinks he's only *pretending* nothing has happened. The truth is, as far as she can figure it, he's been up to no good. He's got something up his sleeve. He is hiding something from her.

This kind of confusion can lead to explosive quarrels,

which can lead to intimate times of making up, which can lead to the man's re-withdrawal from intimacy. It's a dangerous cycle, both hurtful and destructive. Eventually the angry, quarreling words take their toll, the times of intimacy weaken, and the relationship begins to erode.

Understanding the rubber band dynamic is essential to couples, as Dr. Gray points out. "When a man gets too close and doesn't pull away, common symptoms are increased moodiness, irritability, passiveness, and defensiveness.... Understanding this male intimacy cycle is just as important for men as it is for women."[3]

Iron Jane has to come to understand this cycle, and she can even help her mate understand her own difficulties with it. Her advice:

> *If we anticipate his need to pull away, it will be easier to welcome him back.*

TO TALK OR NOT TO TALK?

Sometimes it's difficult to separate social differences from emotional ones. It's a bit like asking "which came first, the chicken or the egg?"

You can be sure of one thing–some things may start out being social, but they'll end up causing major emotional trouble. For example, men and women tend to react differently to difficulties. If you'll permit me to generalize: *Men withdraw from discussing problems; women want to talk about them.*

This situation could well be traced to left brain/right brain distinctions. Or it may have to do with those independence vs. intimacy dissimilarities. Call it what you will, here's how it works.

Carol and Harry have just received word that his company wants to transfer him from Iowa to New York City. The job transfer means a promotion to vice-president, all moving costs covered by the company, a great deal more money, international travel, and a large expense account.

On the down side, it means leaving both sets of parents. It requires taking their three children out of school in the middle of the year. It involves selling the house, finding a new home, saying good-bye to a lifetime of memories and rebuilding a lifestyle.

Both Carol and Harry agree that they can't pass up this golden opportunity. There is no disagreement as far as the decision to move is concerned. But the more Carol tries to talk to Harry about the details and logistics they have to face, the more Harry withdraws.

At first, Carol assumes he's in a bad mood, and she's temporarily understanding. But days pass, and her own fears and insecurities about moving are mounting steadily. She talks to her friends, talks to her mother and Harry's mother, talks to the children, and even talks to her Bible study group.

But she can't seem to talk to Harry.

Harry, in the meantime, is trying to work things out in his mind. He is just as anxious as Carol. Maybe he's even more anxious, because he feels completely responsible for the change. His thinking pattern goes like this: *What if it's a huge mistake? What if I fail in my new job? What if the children's lives are damaged? Is the new house payment too large? What if Carol is unable to cope with the loneliness of a new community?*

On and on his mind races. But he keeps his thoughts to himself.

Carol interrupts his musings. "Harry, can we talk a minute? I've got some major concerns about our move."

You think I don't? he feels like saying. *I've got a lot more to worry about than you do.* But he simply replies, "I don't want to talk about it right now."

Carol thinks, *You don't love me or you'd comfort me. You'd put your arms around me and tell me everything's going to be all right.* Instead, she says, "Honey, why? Don't you understand how much we have to do before we can go? It's going to be really hard, and I'm really worried..."

"Don't worry, it'll all work out." With that, Harry gives Carol a quick peck on the forehead, and heads for the den where he spends the next hour shuffling papers and pretending he's watching the news. When Carol expresses her fears, Harry's worries increase; his own uncertainties deepen.

Why won't Harry talk to Carol? Because he hasn't yet solved the problems of their relocation in his own mind. Like many other men, he likes to work things out first and talk second. He assumes that Carol expects him to have all the answers, and he feels inadequate. Perhaps he even imagines that she's questioning his competence.

Carol, on the other hand, isn't really looking for solutions. She wants to talk things through together, and coming up with answers isn't her first priority. It's intimacy she's after.

LIKE A BEAR IN HIS DEN

Whether a man is being a rubber band because he's so in love it scares him, or whether he's withdrawing to solve a problem, he's being "normal"–for a man. But in either case, when he pulls away, a woman feels shut out, cut off, rejected or abandoned.

Of course, this situation can be completely reversed.

◆ There are extroverted men who talk before they know what to say.

◆ There are angry men who say hurtful things before they think.

◆ There are quiet women who choose their comments sparsely and carefully.

◆ There are depressed women who cannot find words, or the energy to use them, in order to communicate their deepest needs.

But generally speaking, men retreat into their inner sanctums to regroup, and we women all too often rush in after them. We want to rescue them from their pain and we want to reassure ourselves that they still love us.

Unfortunately, we may not be welcomed into their presence at that particular moment. Our kindness may be misinterpreted, our compassion rejected. The bear in his den may snarl at us, sending us out more wounded than when we went in.

> *Men confuse empathy with sympathy because they don't want to be pitied.*

FAMILY INFLUENCES–THE GOOD, THE BAD, THE UGLY

Some social differences between men and women have their roots in their families of origin. Individuals who have grown up in a stressful or addictive environment have usually learned–the hard way–not to talk about problems. They are inclined to keep their feelings to themselves, and perhaps don't even know what's inside their own hearts. "Denial" is the secret password to survival in severely disturbed households.

No matter whether childhood abuse was inflicted by males or females, whether it was sexual or physical or verbal, whether the victim was eighteen months or eighteen years old, family troubles have the capacity to damage future relationships.

People who have been severely injured during childhood have a difficult time trusting others or connecting emotionally when they reach adulthood. Why? Because, as children, when they offered love they received pain. Unconsciously, therefore, they are afraid to love because they equate loving with being wounded. This can make a tremendous difference in the way both men and women form personal, social, and even spiritual connections.

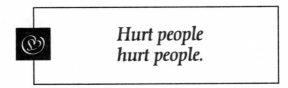

> *Hurt people*
> *hurt people.*

Abuse isn't the only determining factor in the way our families affect us. Role modeling during childhood affects both our adult expectations and the way we play out our own adult roles.

For instance, if we grew up with a father who was forever placating and pleasing our mother, we grow up expecting all men to behave that way. We feel unloved if our husbands don't do the same.

In a similar sense, if our mother was demanding and verbally abusive, we may hear ourselves screaming angry words at our husbands and children. We have to stop, control ourselves, and refuse to repeat the behavior that seemed "normal" to us as children.

Mothers and sons have a particularly unique and complex chemistry. Men's relationships with their mothers are tremendously influential in their marriages, for better or for worse. An understanding of your man's relationship with his mom can help you avoid tripping land mines in your relationship with him.

It is often advised, "Watch to see how your boyfriend treats his mother–if he treats her well, he'll probably be a good husband." On the other hand, if a man grows up with a mother who manipulates him, he may mistrust all women in general, assuming females always have ulterior motives and hidden agendas.

> *Men's relationships with their mothers are tremendously influential in their marriages, for better or for worse.*

In order to understand your man, you'll want to start by hearing about his family. And, if things weren't so good at home, you may have to read between the lines, because his childhood defenses–denial and repression–may not allow him either to remember hurtful incidents or to honestly describe them to you. Our culture is changing rapidly, and families are the prime victims. Sad to say, every generation of damaged kids tends to repeat the unwholesome behavior of the one before.

GREAT EXPECTATIONS

One significant influence in all our lives is that familiar living room appliance with a rectangular screen and a picture tube. Almost every family has at least one television set, and besides our childhood home environment, TV programming is perhaps the most pervasive purveyor of unrealistic male-female role models.

Men in dramatic roles, generally speaking, are presented as strong, independent, and successful leaders. They are often loners, with dominant personalities, good bodies, great charm and no problems that they cannot solve single-handedly. By contrast, men in comedy roles are usually confused, outsmarted by women and children, klutzy, and physically unappealing.

Women in TV dramas are often male-dependent; physically beautiful and intellectually shallow. They provide sexual distraction rather than substantial personal support. Comediennes, in the meantime, are often coarse, male-bashing, and, especially in sitcoms, chronically manipulative and "superior" to their male counterparts.

One of the most damaging notions the media have conveyed to our culture has to do with the concept of love itself. We have been given the idea that being in love is an ongoing romantic dream. According to most scripts, love's excitement never fades, its emotion never diminishes, its ardor never wanes. We've been indoctrinated by songs, movies, novels, and television that if "that lovin' feeling" is no longer present in a relationship, love itself is dead. The relationship is gone, gone, gone and it's time to look for a new leading man or woman. Hollywood has never learned that *love is a decision, not an emotion.*

LEARNING THE WRONG LESSONS

What do male children, adolescents, and even adults learn from twisted families and not-so-great role models? And how does what they learn impact their relationships with women? Dr. Barbara DeAngelis, in her book *Secrets about Men Every Woman Should Know*, offers the following parallel about what men have learned from their families, our culture, and other males they admire, and what women expect from them:

The Way Men Have Been **Taught** *to Be*	*The Way We* **Want** *Men to Be*
Defensive and suspicious	Trusting and open
Hide their emotions	Show their emotions
Competitive	Cooperative
Appear strong and unconquerable	Express their vulnerability
Master the outer world	Master the inner world
Independent/the Loner	Feel their need for us
Stay in control	Let go of control[4]

IN SPITE OF EVERYTHING...

It's always a mistake to generalize when we're talking about men's and women's social differences. I'm reluctant to slot men into one category and to class women in another. We are all so different–I know I'm not a typical female in some ways. Most women prefer to "nest" and be domestic. But I have to admit that my only domestic quality ... is that I live in a house!

While we were discussing vacation destinations, I told Hal, "I want to go somewhere I've never been before."

"Good!" he cheered. "Let's go to the kitchen."

I took the opportunity to remind him that the best thing I make for dinner is reservations.

No two couples share the same set of differences. So how can there be common solutions? There can't. But we can be informed. We can ask questions. We can observe family–of–origin relationships. We can permit his solitude. We can help him understand our yearning for intimacy. We can provide him privacy. We can give one another the benefit of the doubt. We can choose to love–unconditionally.

No matter what the differences may be between you and the man in your life, *understanding* is the first step toward harmony. This is especially true when the disagreements don't involve morality or "right vs. wrong." It's essential for us all to remember the following: no matter how irritated we get,

> *Relationships are more important than differences of opinion.*

Chapter 4

Is He Emotionally Brain Dead?

Five teenage boys clambered into the carpool minivan. They were talking among themselves rather seriously. Kate, the mother of two of the boys and driver of the carpool, was listening carefully.

"Could you believe all those girls crying?" her son Don shook his head in disbelief.

Gene, a neighbor boy, nodded. "There must have been a dozen of them. You could hear them a mile away!"

"Was one of them his girlfriend?"

"Yeah, Marcy was. She was *really* crying loud."

Kate interrupted, "What on earth happened? Why were a dozen girls crying?"

"More than a dozen," Paul, her other son interjected. "I think it was more like fifty. The whole girls' P.E. class was standing in a circle crying."

"But why?"

"Oh, we heard today that Jacob West died in a car accident yesterday. All the girls completely freaked when they heard about it."

There was a brief silence in the car. Kate stole a glance in the rear view mirror at the faces of the boys in the back. They were pale and thoughtful. Both of her sons looked troubled.

"Did you guys know Jacob?"

"Yeah, we knew him. He was a senior, so we didn't hang out or anything. But we knew him."

"Are you upset?"

"Kind of."

"Well, yeah. It's sad."

"I don't know. It's just weird."

Once Kate had dropped the other boys off at their houses, she walked into the house with Paul and Don. They were still unusually quiet. "Can I ask you something?" she said softly.

Paul shrugged. "Sure. What?"

"Do you think the girls felt worse about Jacob's death than the boys did?"

Paul and Don looked at each other. "Of course not," Don answered rather defensively. "Girls just let their feelings show more than boys."

Kate nodded, but she wasn't quite satisfied. "But you guys have always been encouraged to express your feelings. You've seen your Dad cry. Would you be ashamed to cry in front of your friends at school?"

"I wouldn't be ashamed if Jacob was my best friend," Don piped up. "Then I wouldn't care what anybody thought. But girls are different. If one of them cries, they all start crying. Boys just aren't like that."

"Does it bother you when you see them crying?"

"Sort of." Paul looked at his mother. "I guess it makes me feel like I should do something, but I don't know what to do."

"Yeah," Don added. "And I feel like a wimp if I show my feelings like that. I guess I don't understand why it's OK for them and not for me."

Kate looked at her sons, wondering how, when, and where they had learned to respond in such a stereotypical way. She and Jerry, her husband, had tried to create an emotionally honest environment in their home. On more than one occasion, the boys had seen their father cry. They had wept openly in front of both him and their mom without embarrassment or reprimand. But no matter. Now that they were teenagers, both boys had become extremely self-conscious about their emotions. Even with parental permission, they didn't feel free to cry in public because of social mores in their age group.

Don and Paul will grow up to be normal men, perhaps a little more sensitive than some, thanks to their parents' wisdom. But at some point or other, their wives will become frustrated with them, wondering why on earth they are so aloof.

What seems to a woman to be a normal emotional response is very different for the average male. It's just not natural for him to meet up with one of his buddies on the golf course and say, "Hey Bubba, I sense that I'm troubled by a nurturing deficiency. It's probably due to my dysfunctional family–of–origin. Don't you agree?" Get Real!

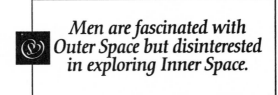

Men are fascinated with Outer Space but disinterested in exploring Inner Space.

WHERE IS HIS HEART?

In our Western culture, most women would say they don't feel emotionally compatible with their men, while most men seem to have a difficult time dealing with emotional women. Women often struggle with this, sensing that they aren't really free to "be themselves" around the males whose comfort would mean the world to them.

At the same time, women don't understand men's seemingly detached and untouchable demeanor. To them, it feels as if the Tin Man from the Wizard of Oz, with no heart inside, has moved into their lives. To make matters worse, these tin men seem quite unaware that something's missing.

Meanwhile, like the teenage girls in the story, most women have learned to weep and mourn when they feel pain. It was acceptable for us to do so as children and adolescents, and it still is culturally proper for us to emote as adults. However, once you find yourself in a close relationship with a man and you take your tears to him, one of several things may happen.

MEN'S REACTIONS TO TEARS

◆ He may give you a quick hug and rush out of the room.

◆ He may order you to stop overreacting.

◆ He may tell you the problem wouldn't have happened if you'd done things differently.

◆ He may provide you with fifteen possible solutions.

◆ He may push the mute button on the TV remote control and stare at you.

◆ He may say, "Calm down, and we'll talk about it when you're feeling better."

◆ He may inquire about whether this is a PMS attack or how close you are to menopause.

◆ He may get angry and shout, "So what did I do this time?"

EMOTIONAL EMISSIONS

Why are women's emotions so traumatizing to men? There are several reasons that the male of the species doesn't deal well with our tears.

For one thing, as we discussed earlier, men are more left brain-oriented. They aren't as intuitive, and therefore their ability to empathize is not well-developed. They don't "feel" what we feel and consequently they genuinely don't understand what we're going through.

Second, men feel threatened when they think their wisdom is being questioned, their credibility assaulted, their strength challenged. It's a male ego issue. More on this later in the chapter.

> *Your conflict may be physiological—not just a personality problem or a difference of opinion.*

Physiological differences tie into the third reason: by virtue of their facts vs. feelings orientation, *men are natural-born problem solvers.* To make matters worse for the women around them, they are taught from their earliest years that they should be able to fix things. So, instead of providing emotional support, they come up with a list of possible actions that will remove the problem, remedy the crisis, and restore contentment.

When you hit a rough spot together, it's worth remembering that your conflict may be physiological–not just a personality problem or a difference of opinion.

CALLING MR. FIX-IT

One night I called home from a hotel. I was away for a speaking engagement, and was looking forward to talking to my loving husband. I remember saying, "I can't wait to get on that plane tomorrow morning. I've had a great time speaking, but I'm really wiped out."

Hal responded as I might have expected, "Get a good night's sleep and you'll feel better."

I continued, "I wish I could. But there's a noisy convention in the hotel. People are partying and slamming doors."

"Change hotels."

"I can't. The people that scheduled me paid for this room. You know, sometimes I wonder why people think traveling is so glamorous..."

"So stay home. Stop traveling. Just write books and speak locally. Learn to cook again."

"Hal, you know better than that. A publisher wants an author who travels and speaks. It's just too bad it had to be this weekend. I'm missing Jan's son's wedding."

"Send a gift. They won't remember."

"But I want to show up and support my friend. I'm there so seldom when my friends need me."

"It's no biggie. They'll understand. Stop beating yourself up–you're blowing everything out of proportion."

Needless to say, I hung up the phone feeling less than comforted. Of course, from Hal's perspective, he was giving me logical answers, trying to keep me from being unnecessarily upset. He was simply flexing his left brain, but I wasn't impressed. I wanted love and affection, not advice.

> *A man feels duty-bound to be "Dr. Dad" to his woman; while a woman feels she is "home schooling" her man.*

A man's inbred predisposition to fix what's wrong puts him under a lot of pressure. He feels less a man if he cannot instantly know what the solution is. His ego is at stake. When his woman talks about a problem, he feels he is responsible to know the answer. Like a Daddy, he feels obligated to come up with the magic solution, so his "little girl" won't fret. You can see how our natural male-female tendencies are at odds with each other.

I feel sorry for males. Their need to always know the answers is the reason they won't stop and ask directions— "I *know* where I'm going, thank you!" Maybe that's why Moses wandered forty years in the wilderness? Even he wouldn't ask directions. And when the car breaks down on the highway, you'll always find the man staring into the engine, even when he hasn't a clue how it works. He has to *appear* to know. All the while his wife is telling him to just put the "HELP" sign in the window and turn the air conditioning back on!

Emotionally, this is where we women get crosswise with our men. We're sure we are in their lives to give them the guidance they so sorely need. Essentially, we're over-eager to give advice too, but for our own set of reasons. And while we're chomping at the bit to provide our brilliant solution to a problem, he is yearning to pull away, to get alone with himself, to examine the situation.

> *His tendency is to analyze first.*
> *Her tendency is to advise first.*

Instead of pushing him, say, "I don't expect you to have all the answers, Honey. I don't require you to be the world's hottest lover, an award-winning electrician and plumber. Let's tackle this together, OK?" Or better still, both of you, take the advice of the Master communicator Jesus Christ: "Give to him who *asks* of thee!" And try to learn how to better explain what you really need.

> *Advice is like snow:*
> *The softer it falls, the deeper it sinks!*

TEARS OF MANIPULATION?

When we're lonely, tired or hurt, we women couldn't care less about brain lobes or male societal norms. We want understanding. At no time does that wonderful quality *intimacy* seem more appealing than when we are feeling blue. Sad to say, there are very few times that men are less likely to provide the closeness we crave than when we are emotionally needy. Men think, *She's crying because she wants me to do something!* That's usually not quite it.

Suzanne sat crying in her bedroom. Hank rushed in to grab his wallet, and found her there. Being a decent sort of guy, he stopped and said, "What's wrong?"

"Nothing."

"Well something must be wrong."

Silence.

"Look, I'm going out to the hardware store. Do you want me to pick anything up for you?"

"No."

"'Bye."

"Hank?"

"Yeah?"

"Why do you always leave the trash for me to take out? You know my back is sore, and it's Saturday so you've got lots of time. And yet you left it for me again today."

"That's why you're crying? Because of the trash? Are you trying to manipulate me?"

Suzanne began to sob in earnest. Hank hesitated, wanting desperately to leave the room. He offered, "I was going to do it later. Why don't you just leave it?"

"Because if I just leave it, it overflows. And then you say I'm manipulating you by letting it overflow. And when I take it out myself, you say I'm manipulating you by carrying the heavy trash out in front of you."

"Oh. Well, just ask me. I'll try to do it when you ask."

"Why should I have to ask?"

"Why should you have to cry over the stupid trash? Look, I'm sorry. And I'll try harder. What more do you want? See you later—I'm off to the Skillsaw sale."

This conversation reflects the very reason I self-published a book entitled, *What Men Understand about Women*... it had nothing in it but blank pages!

At the beginning of the dialogue, Suzanne may have been crying because she was sad. But by the end, tears of frustration and rage had probably mingled with the others, possibly drowning them out. And yet, from Hank's perspective, he was being logical. As far as he was concerned, the trash was no big deal. He hadn't meant to hurt his wife. She just had a different set of priorities than he did.

> *Man's perception:*
> *"She's crying because*
> *she wants me to*
> *do something!"*

Little boys hate doing jobs around the house. This can be proved scientifically by conversations with mothers of sons. Those desperate moms come up with all sorts of ways to motivate their offspring. They threaten. They punish. They pay extra allowance money. They allow ants to infest their son's rooms. They close the door and ignore the mess. Ultimately, given a bad day with lots of other complications, they cry.

Does that kind of emotion amount to manipulation or is it simply unresolved frustration? The fact that moms let their sons see their tears may imply manipulation. Or it may be that they are beyond caring what the lazy little slobs think.

In any case, the sons think "Mom's working me again." They spray the room with Raid, turn MTV on full blast, and close the door. Or if they are of a more sensitive nature, they may shove all the offending debris under the bed or in the closet, apologize, and rush out to play ball.

BEWARE OF "HYSTERICAL" WOMEN!

On one hand, when faced with a weeping woman, a man may be simply unwilling, reacting negatively to what's asked or expected of him. On the other, the poor guy may simply not know what he should do. He's frightened, unsure and unable to function. He can't find the right questions to ask, and he's afraid to say anything, for fear of making a bad situation worse. In his deep confusion, he flips on the Redskins–Rams game.

At that point he may or may not have entered another dreaded arena: *female hysteria.*

Female hysteria is something that looms in the minds of some men like the monsters that lived in the closet when they were toddlers. Perhaps it's only a possible scenario, one they may never have actually witnessed. Or maybe the first wife was histrionic with a solid history in shrieking, wailing, and breaking glass and china against walls. In any case, female hysterics chill the heart of males of every age. They react automatically to an inner urge that says, *If I don't make her stop crying, she'll never stop.*

Barbara DeAngelis writes,

> ... for most men to show strong emotions, such as helplessness or fear, they'd have to be in really bad shape. So when your man sees you really upset about something, he projects his own emotional standards onto you and assumes you must be falling apart! Men don't understand how deeply women can feel about things in the moment without it totally overwhelming their sense of emotional balance.[1]

This brings us to another subject, one which has probably done substantial damage to male-female relationships for generations. Your mother probably mentioned it to you more than once. I know mine did. It is the matter of the male ego.

WHAT IS THE MALE EGO?

Is the "male ego" like "female intuition," a mysterious quality that is used mostly as a weapon in arguments? Or is there something serious at stake here—something real and important both to men and women?

Hal and I were pulling out of the driveway, headed for

a concert in the city. I glanced at my watch. "Boy, I hope the traffic isn't bad, or we'll never make it on time. Did you bring the tickets?"

"Don't I always?" Hal's voice sounded slightly tense.

"I'm just asking. Don't get so ticked." I glanced at the gas gauge. "We'd better stop for gas first."

Hal looked at the gauge himself. "I'll get gas when I need it. This gauge isn't right."

"But we can fill up now, and then we won't have to search for an open station later on."

Hal turned and stared at me. "Do I do this to you when you're driving? Do *you* want to drive?"

I straightened my skirt, and tried not to look smug. "No, but I fill up the tank before we leave. And besides, I don't mind asking directions when I'm lost. That reminds me, should I dig out the map?"

From my point of view, all my questions to Hal were reasonable–I simply wanted him to do things my way, because my way seemed better than his way. But what he heard was something rather different. In that brief conversation, Hal heard me question his memory, his wisdom, his capability and his good sense–all in less than a minute's time.

It's one thing if we want to look at the male ego question from a purely earthbound and secular perspective. In that case, we'd simply assume that men have been running the world for thousands of years, and they therefore think they've earned the right to have their way, to demand their power position and–no matter what else they do–to never be confronted and told that they are wrong. In that light, the "male ego" simply looks like defensiveness, pride, and arrogance.

This is the posture that implies "all men are jerks," all-too-often that of the American feminist. Unfortunately, such a stance doesn't solve anything. It only compounds the problems between men and women.

From a different perspective, we ought to look again at God's original creation. He created the man to be physically stronger, and to move into life with aggressiveness and inner drive. Woman, who was designed to be less physically powerful, has a natural tendency to depend on men for certain difficult tasks, for protection and for leadership. As Dr. Larry Crabb says, she was created to both physically and emotionally "receive" man into her embrace.

Things Difficult for Men:

◆ saying "I'm sorry."

◆ asking for directions.

◆ receiving advice.

◆ graciously responding to being reminded.

◆ discussing differences.

◆ seeking for solutions from outside sources.

◆ understanding when they are denied sex.

SOME THINGS ARE DIFFICULT FOR MEN

Males encounter rough water when they set sail upon the sea of male-female relationships. If you consider that...

> *Men dread overemotionalism.*
> *Men fear their own inadequacy.*
> *Men cling to their independence.*
> *Men hide shame over their*
> *   sexual impulses.*

... it's not hard to imagine that women amount to a major dilemma for men.

The average single man doesn't know how to fit a woman into his life without being completely absorbed by her, and thereby forced into a premature commitment. The average husband, although committed, still struggles to retain his sense of individuality and autonomy.

Why the ambivalence? Because–no matter who she is, what she looks like, or where she's from–the average woman wants a safe and lasting relationship with the man she loves more than anything else. She wants to enjoy him, partner with him, and settle down to unity and contentment.

Of course there are women, especially in today's "liberated" world, who will emphatically deny that they fit into that pattern. Some single women find a second career in male-bashing. Some wives, weary of emotional imbalances, have found happiness in children, careers or other involvements. Nevertheless, for many women, relation-ships with men hold a very important place in their lives.

INTIMACY VS. INDEPENDENCE

Penny studied Dale across the table, and her heart ached. He looked weary, almost ill. For the past four weeks he had been fighting to hang on to his job. He was forty-six years old, and had worked for his company for twenty years. His personal identity was wrapped up in the highly visible position he held there, and at his age, he'd never find another situation to match the one he was about to lose.

Just before the job threat materialized, Penny had found that Dale was infatuated with another woman. So far, it had only amounted to a flirtation, and he had apologetically and tearfully acknowledged that he was extremely vulnerable to such an ego boost. They both blamed the situation on "mid-life crisis." Penny had for-given him, and the two of them had determined to work on the twenty-five-year marriage with all their hearts.

Then Dale's career hit thin ice.

Penny was a sensitive woman, and she understood how devastating this period of time was to him. But she battled every day with insecurities. Night after night, he talked nonstop about the details of his struggles at work. He described one tense scene after another, and related confrontation after confrontation.

Penny listened patiently, but knew deep in her heart that her spouse was treating her more like a friend than a wife. Dale had completely stopped showing her affection. He never asked about her concerns or interests. He was rarely interested in sex.

Nevertheless, she offered whatever encouragement she could. She made his favorite meals, bought him presents, and did all the little extra things women do when they're trying to say "I Love You."

Dale came home every night. He did nothing to arouse suspicion. But questions haunted Penny day and night. Was he still having long lunches with the other woman? Was he pouring out his heart to her when he wasn't talking to Penny? Had his apparently sincere efforts to rebuild the marriage been derailed by the job crisis? Those thoughts almost sickened her.

That night during dinner, when there was a brief pause in his ongoing diatribe about the office, Penny tentatively asked, "Dale, is everything OK between us? I thought we were going to work on our relationship..."

At first Dale just stared at her. Then he answered, his voice cold and hard. "What do you want from me? I have nothing to offer you! Can't you see that I've got more important things on my mind than making you feel secure? My whole world is falling apart!"

Penny fought back her tears, looked at her husband and nodded. "Your job may be your world, Dale, but loving you is mine. My world is falling apart, too."

HIS COMPARTMENTALIZED WORLD

A man devotes his life to his career. He identifies himself by it, he pours his energy into it, and he feels great satisfaction in his success. His woman is important to him, to be sure.

> *A woman fits into a special compartment of a man's heart, but he only visits that compartment when he's not focused on his work.*

She is a precious part of him. He cherishes her, and wouldn't give her up for anything. But, in spite of his commitment to support her and care for her, she is probably *not his primary concern* when he is focused on his workday.

Hence, an insecure wife may ask her husband as he comes through the door, "Did you think of me today, babe?"

"Huh?" he may reply, his face puzzled.

"I know you don't have time to call, but did you think of me today?"

"With my workload? With all I have to do? Are you crazy?"

To make matters more complex, when things aren't going well with a man's career, he feels less lovable. He quickly assumes that he has nothing to offer. He may withdraw from his marriage relationship, if not physically, at least emotionally. He might become unusually irritable and demanding. Nothing a woman does for him pleases him the way she'd like it to; in fact, he probably wishes she'd quit trying so hard. He may or may not still seek sexual intimacy with her, but his heart and mind are else-where.

Meanwhile, many women have only one compartment in their heart, and a special man lives there. Everything else in her world orbits around him. She may be success-ful, she may be socially active, she may be a busy mother or a powerful executive. But the relationship with her man is like a warm sun that brightens her world. And when it is clouded by misunderstanding, estrangement or separa-tion, she lives with a cold shadow eclipsing her happiness.

EXCEPTIONS TO THE RULE

Of course there are always people who don't fit the mold.

◆ Some men become compulsively addicted to relation-ships with women.

◆ Some women are terrorized by their man's emotional-ism and completely shut down their own feelings.

◆ Some men are far more open to growth, suggestions, and "being wrong" than the proud, self-righteous women they love.

◆ Some feminists wouldn't ask a man for the time of day.

◆ Some males are so dependent on women that they've lost their ability to compete or excel.

◆ Some wounded females mistrust all men and sabotage

every relationship that comes their way.

◆ Some men are misogynists who despise women, drawing them just close enough to punish them for being female.

But most mature adults can see in themselves many elements of the more typical stereotypes of men and women.

DIFFERENT EMOTIONAL PRIORITIES

Barbara DeAngelis explains, "Men define themselves primarily from *their work* and their accomplishments; women define themselves primarily from *their relationships.*"[2]

Deborah Tannen writes, "Though all humans need both *intimacy and independence*, women tend to focus on the first and men on the second. It is as if their lifeblood ran in different directions."[3]

John Gray states, "When a man does not feel needed in a relationship, he gradually becomes passive and less energized; with each passing day *he has less to give the relationship....* When a woman does not feel cherished in a relationship she gradually becomes compulsively responsible and *[she becomes] exhausted from giving too much.*"[4]

Generally speaking, and of course there are notable exceptions, men and women view the relationship journey from entirely different viewpoints. Amazingly, however, love comes along anyway. And when it begins to bud, blossom, and flourish, that's the time to begin the endless job of listening and learning. Do you know how he feels? Teach him to tell you. Let him know how you feel and why. Most importantly, perhaps, allow him to be himself. Give him permission to feel different emotional responses than you do.

After all, he's a man, isn't he?

 Love is a decision, not an emotion.

Chapter 5

Who Needs What?

The young couple sat in a quiet restaurant. It was the second or third time they'd been out together and they both sensed that something wonderful was happening between them. They were of the same mind spiritually, so when their meal was served, David took Becky's hand, smiled at her warmly and began to bless the food.

She listened to his words, deeply touched by the sweetness of the moment. Tears burned her eyes as her companion thanked the Lord for their friendship, and prayed his blessing upon them and their dinner. And then he said, "And Lord I pray that you'll meet Becky's needs, and I pray that you'll meet mine."

Becky never forgot the words David prayed, and as

the two of them moved through their courtship into marriage, she sometimes silently said, "Father, remember Dave's prayer. Please meet his needs, and please meet mine."

Not once did she ask herself, nor inquire of her husband-to-be, just exactly what he'd had in mind as he prayed. *She assumed that their needs were the same.* And she innocently imagined that if she kept the "golden rule," doing for Dave what she wanted done for herself, their marriage would work perfectly.

Unfortunately, she couldn't have been more mistaken.

Just as men and women have different bodies, different ways of communicating, different sexual drives, and different priorities in life, they also have unique needs. It is rather shocking to see, listed in order, the things men feel they need, and a comparative itemization of women's necessities. We'll look at several of those lists in a few minutes. But first, let's look on the light side.

Men sure need *women*—even in the bathroom, where their aim isn't so good. Somebody's got to keep things cleaned up. To make matters worse, do you know how many men it takes to change a roll of toilet paper? Nobody knows—it has never happened.

Men also need women as fashion consultants. Many men are helpless when it comes to dressing. Why is it that large numbers cannot dress themselves? So many can't even pick out a belt or determine whether a tie and sox match.

As far as female needs go, Sofie Tucker may have been right:

> *From birth to 18, a girl
> needs good parents;
> from 18-35 she needs good looks;*
> *from 35-55 she needs a
> good personality;
> from 55 on she needs good cash!*

Occasionally my husband and I conduct couples classes on meeting our very different needs. It isn't uncommon to observe a woman elbowing her husband from time to time. It is as if she is saying, "See? Even the experts say you're a jerk."

Do men make the best jerks? How about women? Or... could it be we're just *different?*

Our differences show up in the way we respond to various situations.

Reaction to being out of work:
  Woman: I'm out of work now. I'm looking for another job.
  Man: I have a deal pending.... I'm waiting to hear back.

Reaction to car problems:
  Woman: Put a sign in the window and look for a road-side phone.
  Man: Open the hood. Look like you know what you're doing. Once you get the car home, sell it.

When buying a house:
Woman: Check only two things—the closets and the kitchen.
Man: Take a tape measure into every room.

Idea of a romantic evening:
Woman: Flowers and dinner out.
Man: Stay home, order pizza, and rent the movie, *The Terminator.*

FOUR BASIC HUMAN NEEDS

Before we begin to consider specific needs, let's remind ourselves that there are some things in life we want—but those wants really shouldn't be qualified as needs. It's important to know the difference between needs and wants.

Of course we know that everyone needs food, clothing, shelter and the basic necessities of life. In addition, even though men and women aren't the same physically, emotionally or culturally, males and females do share some other requirements.

We know that there are needs that both sexes—all human beings—want, long for, desire. If we are to be healthy in every way, we do in fact *need* them.

Human Need #1: Common courtesy and respect. This requirement is equally applicable to either sex. Everyone everywhere yearns to be handled with kindness, grace, and patience. An irony that should be obvious to most of us is that the people closest to us are frequently the ones we treat with the most cruelty. This is because our phoniness wears off with them–they see us as we really are. Sadly, the way we really are isn't always a pretty picture.

Human Need #2: Unconditional love. When we offer love in order to get something for ourselves, we aren't really loving at all. We are bartering affection or manipulating.

When we love out of duty, we aren't really loving–we're playing a role.

When we love because the other person seems perfect in our eyes, we're living in a fantasy, about to be disappointed.

But when we love our imperfect, flawed, and difficult-to-love partners of the opposite sex, we are meeting a need that is common to human beings of all ages. We are loving them in spite of their weaknesses, not simply because of their strengths.

Human Need #3: Unselfishness. Self-centered, self-gratifying, self-absorbed men are lethal to women. And the opposite is equally true. Selfish women destroy men. When Jesus taught us to love our neighbor as we love ourselves, he surely didn't mean to look only to the folks next door or down the street, or the strangers across town. He meant for us to practice this great commandment day after day on the precious loved ones closest to us.

As psychologist Larry Crabb writes, "More than any-thing else, what gets in the way of getting along is *self-cen-teredness that seems reasonable.* God does his deepest work in making us more truly loving when we more clearly see how utterly ugly our selfishness is."[1]

Human Need #4: To forgive and be forgiven. The Lord's Prayer is certainly an intercession without sexual differentiation. When Jesus taught us to ask the Father to "forgive our debts as we forgive our debtors," he was speaking of a global human necessity.

Forgiveness, in fact, is an essential factor in common courtesy. It is a component in unselfishness. And it is a primary element in unconditional love. We cannot stay in a relationship for long without needing to be forgiven, and without forgiving. This is the price we pay for being flawed and sinful men and women.

SOME AMAZING DIFFERENCES

Beyond these four generic requirements, however, there are some needs that seem to be unique to men, and others that are specific to women. To catalogue such necessities always involves the risk of generalization. Nonetheless, let's consider some of the studies done by researchers. The fol-lowing inventory is provided by Willard Harley, Jr in his book *His Needs, Her Needs:*

The man's five most basic needs in marriage are:
1. Sexual fulfillment
2. Recreational companionship

3. An attractive spouse
4. Domestic support
5. Admiration

The woman's five most basic needs in marriage are:
1. Affection
2. Conversation
3. Honesty and openness
4. Financial support
5. Family commitment[2]

Dr. John Gray, in *Men Are from Mars, Women Are from Venus*, provides a different list. He writes,

1. She needs *caring* and he needs *trust*.
2. She needs *understanding* and he needs *acceptance*.
3. She needs *respect* and he needs *appreciation*.
4. She needs *devotion* and he needs *admiration*.
5. She needs *validation* and he needs *approval*.
6. She needs *reassurance* and he needs *encouragement*.[3]

As you can see, in virtually every case, men and women are looking for something different from each other. Not only is there tremendous variation in the requirements of each sex, but frequently these very needs become the primary catalysts in quarrels, the roots of bitterness, and the issues at the core of anger and resentment.

THE GREAT EXCHANGE

If you could read men and women's minds, this is what you might be hearing:

Her: It's hard for me to enjoy our sex life. He refuses to hug me, kiss me, or hold me close without grabbing here, squeezing there, and then dragging me off to the bedroom. He's a slam-bam-thank-you-ma'am kinda guy. And I'm saying "No, thank you!"

Him: It's pretty difficult for me to maintain my affectionate feelings for a woman who acts like a Frigidaire. You could get frostbite in our bedroom.

Her: I wouldn't mind being at my lover's side while he's watching sports on TV, but every time I ask him a question, he gets mad and tells me not to bother him till halftime.

Him: I'd like to enjoy my wife's company on a fishing trip, but she talks so much that she chases all the trout upstream.

Her: I want my husband to be truthful and open with me, but honesty has its limits. He's always reminding me that I'm too fat, too tired-looking, or too old. My interest in him and his honesty is fading–big time!

Him: I have a hard time being forthright and open with a woman who refuses to take care of her physical appearance. She used to look awesome, but nowadays she's beginning to remind me of my Great-Aunt Sophie.

Her: If he thinks "a man's home is his castle," he'd better be willing to earn enough of a king's ransom to pay for it.

Him: If she wants me to bring home the bacon, she'd better be willing to fry it up for me in a pan–and clean the kitchen afterward.

Her: If he wants my approval, he'd better learn to change diapers, take out garbage, and vacuum.

Him: If she wants me to spend time with her and the kids, she'd better stop comparing me with Kevin Costner, Tom Cruise, and her brother-in-law, the wimp.

CLOSENESS VS. COMPETITIVENESS

In *Men Are from Mars, Women Are from Venus,* Dr. John Gray describes his observations regarding the needs of men and women. In his view, women, who focus their lives on relationships, yearn for *care, understanding, respect, devotion, validation, and reassurance.* These needs reflect the receptivity of women; they mirror a female's successful function as a nurturer. They are related to **intimacy.**

Meanwhile, the man's focus is on his achievements outside the home, his competitive edge and his inner drive to succeed. *Trust, acceptance, appreciation, admiration, approval, and encouragement* are reflections back to him of his **independence.**

Whatever male and female needs turn out to be within each individual couple's relationship, they can successfully be met in the context of marriage. And, in the process of meeting them for each other, a couple can become deeply bonded for a lifetime. But sometimes needs fail to be met, for men and women alike, and unmet needs often lead to a major problem.

WHAT CAUSES INFIDELITY?

Whether our needs are for food, drink and shelter, or for emotional, sexual or intellectual companionship, they have one thing in common: when they are unsatisfied, they make us feel deep hunger and driving thirst. Hungry and thirsty people can become distressed and irrational in their craving. In their desperation they sometimes try to meet their own needs in inappropriate ways. Deep thirst can drive us to drink from unhealthy waters.

Why do husbands and wives get involved in extra-marital affairs? Why do couples grow weary of each other and begin to look elsewhere for satisfaction? We've all heard the usual lines: "My wife doesn't understand me." Or, "My husband just isn't there for me."

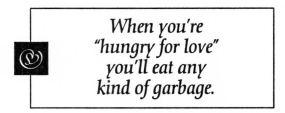

When you're "hungry for love" you'll eat any kind of garbage.

One reason for unfaithfulness between lovers or spouses is that age-old human notion that the grass is always greener on the other side of the fence. There are both men and women who always leave "the back door open," hoping a perfect, unblemished lover will appear–a fantasy-to-end-all-fantasies.

One of the primary reasons that marital compatibility is worth fighting for is because the alternatives are so devastating. Better to solve problems while they're small than to face major estrangement, unfaithfulness, and eventual divorce–and to carry those same problems into subsequent relationships.

THE UNSTABLE WORLD OF FEELINGS

An alternate cause of infidelity is that once we have something, we're inclined to devalue it–the chase is more exciting than the ownership. As James Dobson writes in *What Wives Wish Their Husbands Knew about Women,* "We crave that which we can't attain, but we disrespect that which we can't escape."[4] In other words, you want what you can't have, and you don't appreciate the things that are permanently yours.

Both men and women have cycles in life, whether they are hormonal, triggered by inner emotional changes, or related to outside circumstances. When two people are in a relationship, these cycles rarely coincide. "Feelings" may rise or fall inside one partner, and the reasons might well have nothing to do with anyone else. However, once a partner's restlessness becomes apparent, the other person begins to react.

When a man feels his wife slipping away from him, he

reflexively starts clinging to her. His expressions of jealousy increase, he wants more sex, and he feels paranoid and insecure. Chances are, she will react to his panic by withdrawing even further from him.

Women, according to most researchers, are even more inclined toward clinging. Because we are, generally speaking, highly focused on our personal relationships, we feel a tremendous sense of panic when intimacy with a loved one is threatened. With this in mind, Dr. Dobson's wise advice is to preserve our human dignity always, no matter how desperately we want to keep our loved ones attached to us.

When relationship imbalances occur, men and women begin to think about their needs. They start dwelling on the empty places they feel inside, and often realize that the things they want most in a relationship are the very things they lack. At this point, if we don't communicate about our needs with our partners, we may look in the wrong places to get those needs met.

HOW TO DEAL WITH UNMET NEEDS

So what should we do when we aren't getting what we want out of our relationships?

1. **Take enough time to figure out what's lacking.** Looking at the lists at the beginning of the chapter may provide some ideas, but every person has his or her own unique needs. Make your own list of relationship priorities.

2. **Find the right occasion to communicate** those needs. (I hope you'll read chapter six, about communication, before you do.) Don't be afraid to make waves–little ripples could prevent a tidal wave later on.

3. **Listen** to your partner without being defensive.

4. **Be determined to negotiate** for the benefit of both of you. Meeting mutual needs is a team effort.

5. **Agree on a time for daily or weekly check-ups,** "How am I doing?" dialogues, which will help both of you stay on track.

6. After you've proven to each other that the needs in question are being met on a consistent basis, **celebrate your success** with a weekend away or a dinner out.

SENSIBLY SINGLE

Men and women who are still "unclaimed treasures," still looking for a partner, would be wise to think through their priorities *before* getting deeply involved. Sexual attraction is strong magic, and it sometimes blinds us to reality.

I was single until I was twenty-nine, and wondered how I'd ever snag my man. I could almost picture my tombstone:

> *Here lie the bones of poor old Lee.*
> *Her life it held no terrors.*
> *An old maid she lived,*
> *an old maid she died;*
> *no hits, no runs, no errors.*

Hal and I met Mei Ling in Waikiki. She was a lovely Hawaiian-Chinese waitress, working two jobs to hold things together as a single parent. She'd never known what it was to have child support for the kids, and if she were honest, she'd say she was glad she didn't have anything to do with her ex anymore. She'd rather struggle along without the hassle of dealing with him.

But after eight years of singleness, she was wondering if she'd ever find a man willing to count the cost and make a commitment to her and the kids. She had concluded it was an impossibility. She'd lost confidence in her ability to make a man happy; she still didn't understand males. She told us that she had made up her mind just to keep her nose to the grindstone, and to reconsider the issue once the kids were grown and gone. Maybe her body would still be intact by then...

I see the Mei Lings of the world as potential Iron Janes. They feel the need and the desire for a man, but don't want to volunteer for another failure. They wonder, *was it really better to have loved and lost than never to have loved at all?*

With the boost of some helpful information, coupled with some determination, they *can* enjoy new confidence!

THE RISKS OF BEING A "PLEASER"

Whether we're looking for a new love or working at making things right with a husband, trying desperately to please is a danger. Being a "pleaser" causes us to stop being honest about our own needs in our heroic attempts to satisfy our partner. We've heard so much about giving 100 percent to our partner that we forget they're supposed to be giving 100 percent back to us.

Barbara DeAngelis describes the biggest mistake women make with men. "Women sacrifice who they are and put themselves second in importance to the man they love." She explains that we do this in four dangerous ways:

◆ We give up our own interests, hobbies and activities.

◆ We give up friends or family members our partner doesn't approve of.

◆ We become emotional chameleons, walking into the relationship like a blank slate, and becoming whatever the man wants us to be.

◆ We give up our own dreams in order to help a man make his dreams come true.[5]

This is all wrong! This isn't Iron Jane–it's Wilma the Wimp. It doesn't take a graduate degree in psychology to figure out that once we make those kinds of personal concessions, we end up resentful, cheated, and burned out. We trade in our very selves in order to appeal to somebody else's personality.

Some women have become masters of this game. This is the reason for the popular (and tragic) comment often made about mid-life divorces:

"Men leave women to find other women; women leave men to find themselves."

Whether we're single, dating, married, widowed or divorced, let's take the time to ask God to reveal to us who we really are. He can help us to recognize just what it is that we need, to understand the character of the unique woman he designed us to be.

Once we've taken the time to know ourselves and to treat our deepest needs with respect, we'll be better equipped to consider the needs of others. Most specifically, we'll have more to offer when faced with the deep, unmet needs of the man we love.

Chapter 6

First Things First

Tom and Lynda sat staring at each other across the restaurant table. Neither one of them had touched the plates of food in front of them–they were too upset to eat. Months of domestic tension had finally brought them to a crisis–and a crossroads. Lynda wanted to separate from Tom, at least for a while, until she "found herself again." But Tom didn't want to lose his wife or his children.

"How did it come to this?" Tom quietly asked, almost to himself. "I worked so hard…"

"*You* worked hard?" Lynda's was appalled. "*You?* You got

up, went out the door every morning and disappeared for ten hours. When you got home, I fed you, you crashed in front of the television and fell asleep. In the meantime, I was taking care of your three preschoolers, cleaning your house, washing your clothes, taking your car in for servicing, cooking your meals, ironing your shirts, answering your mail..."

"Now hold it! Hold it just a minute, little lady. What do you think I was doing during those ten hours when you thought I disappeared?"

"You were hanging out with the guys at work, organizing football pools, talking about sports trivia and going to lunches on your expense account."

Tom's voice was stiff and condescending. "Lynda, for your information, I have a job that I go to every day. It's an important job, and I have to work overtime when I have projects to complete. And I make a good living, in case you hadn't noticed. The reason I'm tired when I get home is because I've been killing myself trying to earn a living to support *you*... you and my children. Believe me, you don't work any harder than I do. And furthermore, if I didn't work hard, you wouldn't have any food to cook, any clothes to wash, any house to clean..."

"You just don't get it, do you? Your family is supposed to come first..."

"My family *does* come first. Why do you think I'm working all the time?"

"If your family came first, you'd be spending time with us."

"If I spent more time with you, none of us would be eat-ing! Maybe you'd like to support the family for a while..."

On and on the conversation went. Tom felt outraged by Lynda's inference that he wasn't a good family man. He felt that his whole life was devoted to providing for his family. To make matters worse, their sex life was nonexistent. Lynda looked like a frump most of the time, and she was forever nagging him about his insensitivity.

Lynda thought Tom was an insensitive boor because he gave her "no support at home." He was "too tired" at night to change diapers, empty trash cans or listen to her tales of motherhood. She hadn't had a haircut, a manicure, or a trip to the mall in six months. Worst of all, he was completely unaffectionate, and she couldn't remember the last compliment he'd paid her.

Both Tom and Lynda were marital martyrs. They seemed to be giving their all, and yet both felt unappreciated, unloved, and misunderstood. The primary reason for their conflict was a difference in priorities. Such disparity causes both partners to wear blinders.

If Tom had showed up early at the door the next night with flowers and candy, Lynda might actually have responded, "Oh no, this is a nightmare! The baby's been fussy all day, I feel like I'm getting the flu, the sink is stopped up again, and now you come home drunk!"

IMPOSSIBLE DEMANDS

I guess we women are notorious in the eyes of men for having lists of emotional demands. One frustrated man expressed it this way:

THE RULES

1. The female ALWAYS makes the rules.

2. The rules are SUBJECT TO CHANGE without prior notification.

3. The female is NEVER wrong.

4. If the female appears to be wrong, it is because of a FLAGRANT MISUNDERSTANDING which was a direct result of something the male did or said wrong.

5. If rule 4 applies, the male must APOLOGIZE immediately for causing the misunderstanding.

6. The female can CHANGE HER MIND at any given point in time.

7. The male must NEVER change his mind without express written consent from the female.

8. The female has EVERY RIGHT to be angry or upset at any time.

9. The male must remain CALM AT ALL TIMES, unless the female WANTS him to be angry or upset.

10. If the female has PMS, all rules are null and void.

   (used by permission of A.T. Random Publications)

NEEDS BECOME PRIORITIES

With that thought-provoking list of grievances in mind, let's move (carefully) forward into the subject of men's and women's priorities. In the last chapter, we took a look at what men and women need in their relationships. As we saw, when asked to inventory their primary requirements, males and females didn't list any of the same things. To complicate things further, each assumed that he or she shared an identical set of needs with the other.

Of course it's a very short leap between a need and a priority. When we haven't eaten all day, we need food. And before long that need is driving us—we're soon peering into the fridge or the pantry, or driving ourselves to the nearest Burger King. Food has stopped being a need, and it has become a priority. Note: *Unmet needs become priorities.*

One of the primary reasons it is important for men and women to identify their needs to each other is to prevent the kind of craving that drives them to satisfy those needs with inappropriate behavior. Sometimes we aren't even consciously aware that we are being driven by unmet needs until we've made unwise choices or "acted out."

> ## *Unmet needs become priorities.*

It doesn't require a tremendous amount of imagination to envision what happens to a man when his sexual needs aren't met. Or to a woman when she hasn't felt any affection for a very long time. In short, our needs are the parents of our priorities.

And that's OK, as long as we have our priorities in the

right order. Yet even when we manage to set our priorities in our own minds, we may find ourselves in a battle zone with our partners.

Guess why?

> ***Different sexes have different needs.***
> ***Different needs trigger different priorities.***

THE NATURAL ORDER OF THINGS

When we consider that most women are more relationship-oriented than their men, it's easy to see that their priorities are going to have to do with personal interaction. Like Lynda, a woman's world often revolves around her man, her children, and her friends.

This, of course, doesn't mean that some women aren't highly motivated in their careers. It simply means that, by and large, women are going to prioritize their lives around relationships, connections, and interaction. Unfortunately Lynda, who really wanted her relationship with Tom to be top priority, was shooting herself in the foot with all her miserable manipulation.

Men, as a rule, are more competitive, hierarchical, and focused on their work. There are inevitably exceptions to this statement, but countless men have their own priorities clearly in mind without seeming to grasp their woman's primary concerns. Like Tom, many men feel they are giving their utmost to their families by working long hours. However, they miss the point entirely that their loving presence is just as precious as a fat paycheck. (If it's not asking too much, a little of each would be nice!)

PERSONAL PRIORITIES

Of course, in a broad spectrum, beyond the realm of male-female differences, individuals have their own array of interests and concerns that also become relationship issues.

Carl wanted to be a professional musician. He was taking both voice lessons and sight-reading lessons while rehearsing and vocalizing two hours a day. He had established a group of musician friends who comprised a tight little fraternity. Some of them had more bookings than others, but they all shared the same concern: when would the phone ring with a recording session or a performance opportunity?

When Cheryl met Carl, she was fascinated by his talent and wholeheartedly excited about his future. She saw him as a man with a vision, one who was doing all he could do to get ahead in the career of his choosing. The fact that he was thirty-one and still living with his mother didn't phase Cheryl. It was just a good financial decision, he had quickly explained.

Determined to have a super relationship with her charming, good-looking musician, Cheryl began to help Carl out. When she learned that his mother refused to do his laundry, Cheryl cheerfully took it home with her. When she discovered that he was behind in his credit card payments (it had been a bad summer in the music business), she happily extended him a loan. When he told her that he found her sexually exciting, she invited him to live with her.

From time to time, Carl had great success with his music. He wisely (in Cheryl's eyes) invested whatever extra money he earned in rehearsal tapes, sound equipment, and performance clothing.

Cheryl, in the meantime, had taken a better-paying job to help support the two of them while Carl "got his career moving."

To her delight, Carl asked her to marry him. She said yes, and promptly purchased their set of matching wedding rings herself–Carl had just spent his last $300 on a new amplifier.

Five years went by. Cheryl was vice-president of her corporation. She had grown cynical about Carl's career. He had enjoyed a brief national tour as back-up singer to a pop star, then had returned home to an empty calendar.

Gradually, feeling shamed because of his lack of success and Cheryl's very evident dissatisfaction, Carl became a reluctant house husband, doing the marketing, cleaning, and laundry. She, in turn, was the breadwinner, wrapped up in her career, her projects, and her colleagues.

She had started out with a relationship priority.

He had started out with a career priority.

They ended up with a legal priority–how quickly can a lawyer get us out of this miserable marriage?

Of course there were many factors in Cheryl and Carl's failed marriage. We'll talk about some of them in future chapters–communication, selfishness, and loss of personal boundaries. But it's worth remembering–a relationship that began with unbalanced priorities ended in marital collapse.

PRIORITIES COMMON TO ALL OF US

Are there some priorities that are known ingredients in *every* successful relationship?

It's interesting to talk to people of various religious backgrounds. No matter what their denominational allegiance or their cultural tradition, they will somehow state a nearly universal precept:

The stronger the vertical relationship, the stronger the horizontal relationship. The more you love and honor God, the more you'll love and honor people.

People who discuss the Bible find countless points of disagreement. And yet it is with uncanny repetition that pastor after pastor, teacher after teacher, writer after writer and Christian after Christian list the same set of priorities for successful living:

Priority #1: God
Priority #2: Spouse
Priority #3: Children
Priority #4: Career
Priority #5: Friends and Loved Ones

This list has no gender difference. Once that hierarchy of issues is in place, the rest is up to you (and your partner, if you have one). Perhaps establishing priorities is a process you'll do over a period of time. Or maybe you already know what you wish to pursue together. It may be painful, but it may be fun.

It's not unusual for either partner to get the idea that he or she has slipped way down the priority scale–I came to see that, for a while, I had left Hal dangling off the end of the list. With my press of responsibilities involved in raising children, he had tumbled down to #7 or #8 in importance.

When I finally realized what had happened, I went to a trophy shop to solidify my determination to make things right. I returned home with a giant blue "FIRST PLACE" ribbon which I pinned on him, restating my commitment to honor him above all others. I must admit that I quickly (and I hope tactfully) added that I wanted to be granted the same rank on his list. He wore the ribbon to bed; we were both relieved that we had communicated about our misplaced priorities.

SHARING PRIORITIES

"Is it possible to share his priorities without losing myself?" This is a question many women have asked themselves after experiencing years of quiet desperation and lonely servitude. Whether we start out by clarifying our mutual priorities at the beginning of a relationship, or find it necessary to do so later on, clearly defined priorities in relationships help prevent hurtful conflicts.

By going through the process of defining our relationship priorities, we remove the cause of much grief and turmoil. We can establish priorities through developing a fresh awareness of six considerations.

Relationship Priorities:

◆ Common interests

◆ Conversation

◆ Concern

◆ Compromise

◆ Cooperation

◆ Communion

COMMON INTERESTS

Common interests, along with physical attraction, ought to be the magnets that draw us to our counterparts of the opposite sex in the first place. Unless at the outset of the relationship we are blindly intoxicated entirely by sexual fascination, we should soon find our partner to be our good, if not best, friend. Besides enjoying one another's company, we will probably also be sharing hours of dialogue about things we mutually enjoy.

If, in fact, this isn't the case with your dating or marriage relationship, you'd better hoist a red flag and shout "time out!" A love affair without friendship as its foundation will not survive.

When we bring common interests into a relationship, and continue, over the course of time, to weave them into our daily lives, we can create an environment that fosters working together toward common priorities, not pulling against each other in competition.

Do, however, beware of the kind of relationship my friend Judy sadly reported to me one day: "Jerry and I have so much in common, Lee.... We're both in love with Jerry."

CONVERSATION

Priorities are important—that's a given. And discovering them requires communication—that's an undeniable fact.

It's a sad fact that many men and women, particularly those of religious faith, cling to a superstitious belief that "things will just work out," or that "love conquers all." This often prevents them from addressing controversies. They'd rather talk about pleasant things, saying, "it'll work out eventually, so why rock the boat?" Not so!

Once couples grasp the vital significance of shared priorities, they are more likely to take the time to discuss, debate, and decide upon the things they will put first in their lives, and the things they will set aside if necessary.

Of course communication skills do not come naturally. A wealth of wisdom can be acquired from published sources; I have tried to distill some of this wisdom in chapter seven. Above all, remember: practice makes perfect!

CONCERN

Concern for others is the opposite of self-concern. Seems like I'm stating the obvious, doesn't it? But reflect a moment on how often human beings are blind to their own selfishness, and how often our self-centeredness defeats us in the long run!

Dr. Larry Crabb says, "Self-centered living is the real culprit in marriages with problems. Other-centered living is the answer. Understanding how badly we need forgiveness and celebrating its rich availability moves us in the right direction."[1]

If we are genuinely concerned with the interests, goals, and needs of our partners–and if that concern has no self-serving, hidden agendas–we are on our way to establishing mutually agreeable priorities that can be understood and supported.

> *We should give our partner's priorities the same consideration we give our own.*

A generation of people has learned to "look out for yourself," at the expense of interpersonal intimacy. Of course a measure of self-acceptance, self-respect, and even self-love are necessary for us to have the ability to reach out to others. But in a world so focused on self-gratification, we should give our partner's priorities the same consideration we give our own.

We would be wise to recall the words of Jesus Christ, "Love your neighbor as you love yourself" (Matthew 22:39) and those of the apostle Paul, "Let each of you look not only to his own interests, but also to the interests of others" (Philippians 2:4).

COMPROMISE

Some of our mothers taught us that compromise was a dirty word—it meant giving up our values or cheating on our morals. But when it comes to establishing priorities in a relationship, compromise is essential. It means giving a little here and gaining a little there. It means offering up a piece of our little world in order to benefit the big picture.

Compromise takes us back to the idea of unselfishness, and reminds us that when we've both agreed to give something up, we do it willingly and joyfully. In the religious traditions of the ancient Hebrews, the people were told to sacrifice the best of their flocks in order to demonstrate to their God that he was their first priority. In a far smaller way, when we sacrifice some prize of our own for the good of a precious relationship, it reminds us that we are to live and love beyond ourselves.

A word of warning, however, about compromise: it is important that we don't fall victim to controlling personalities. Women who tend to be pleasers have a hard time standing their ground and saying, "I have my priorities, too, you know." The same goes for some men. We need to remind ourselves, "I don't have to sacrifice *me* to be loved by *you.*"

Compromise doesn't equal passivity nor is it a "give-till-it-hurts" proposition. It's mutual. It's reasonable. It's freely given, with mature love.

It's not worth it to compromise our integrity until we "hit bottom." The consequences of always giving in—the feelings of victimization, the loss of self-respect, and the eventual burn-out—will force us to do what we should have done sooner. It takes courage and conviction to defend our own interests in the face of a not-so-generous partner.

COOPERATION

There is an element of push-pull in every relationship. In many cases, there is one partner who eventually submits to the other, either in fear, in resignation, or in desire to please. Cooperation means taking a firm hold of the power vs. love tension in our relationship, facing up to it and finding a middle ground.

As David and Janet Congo say in their thought-provoking book *The Power of Love,* "As we try to live out our daily lives in reliance on our own strength and wisdom, we will inevitably be either controlled or controlling. Powerful love is the natural consequence of communion with God and with his people. As we let God have more of us, He is ready to give us more of himself."[2]

We ourselves often want to remain at the controls. We want to call the shots personally. We want to come out as winners. Cooperation means letting go of the controls, giving that job to God.

In addition, cooperation means letting go of the habitual compliance that may have characterized our part of the relationship. It means facing up to issues, finding the selflessness to negotiate an agreement, and cheerfully biting the bullet together.

That requires lots of love, not so much the warm fuzzy kind as the tough, courageous kind. God himself is the source of the love between us.

COMMUNION

Once our priorities are established, agreed upon, and mutually supported, our relationships with ourselves, with our partners, and with the world around us will become healthier That brings us to true communion.

We remember that whatever our priorities are, we would be wise to communicate before, during, and after any conflict arises. But like the effort to establish priorities, communication is another battle-zone. Before you go charging into it, flags flying, you may want to call for a ceasefire, take a deep breath and read the next chapter.

> *Clearly defined priorities in relationships help prevent harmful, relational conflicts.*

Chapter 7

What Are You Talking About?

The cartoon says it all. George is sitting in his Barcalounger, absorbed in the game on TV.

Marge is standing next to him. She says, "And after I finished making love to the plumber, he asked me to marry him. I said 'yes,' so we're leaving tomorrow for an around-the-world cruise together. Once I've divorced you and put the kids in boarding school, he and I are getting married in Nassau and starting life over in the Bahamas."

George responds, while flipping channels on the remote, "That's nice, Hon. I'm glad you had a good day."

In spite of this caricature, there is hope for women who live with men who won't listen and won't talk. Most uncommunicative men aren't stubborn; they are uninformed and unpracticed in articulating their feelings.

ENLIGHTEN YOUR MAN

As a thank you to a sweet waitress in a coffee shop, I gave her a copy of my blank book, *What Men Understand about Women.* She laughed with me, but returned thoughtfully to the table remarking, "You know it just occurred to me that this book could save my marriage."

I was tempted to laugh, but her sincere look assured me that this was no joke.

She continued, "Really, if I accept the fact that *this* is true (holding up my blank book), that men just don't understand, then I've got to make it my job to tell my husband what matters. I've got to spell out what I like and don't like. I have to inform him that birthdays are important to me; that I really need him to look me in the eye when we're talking. I guess it's up to me. I shouldn't expect him to read my mind. Thanks so much!"

> *Uncommunicative men aren't stubborn; they are uninformed and unpracticed in articulating their feelings.*

The ball's in our court, gals. If men genuinely don't get it, let's grant them the benefit of the doubt. We can take the communication responsibility to spell out what we need, what we want, what we think, and what we feel. We've assumed too much by expecting them to read our minds. Let's give them a piece of it!

Let's let them know, in no uncertain terms, what hurts us. Do you feel intimidated? When his tone of voice injures something inside you, don't shrink from the battle, Iron Jane. Inform. Discuss. Enlighten. It may sound like this:

◆ I guess you're not aware of how much you hurt me last night. I don't think it was intentional, but it still hurt.

◆ If you don't allow me to express my feelings without walking out of the room or exploding, I'll continue to shrink back from you. Eventually I'll stop trying and caring. Neither of us wants that.

◆ I'm not as strong as you think I am. I can't "take anything." Although I'm getting stronger, I don't want to become hard and insensitive just so you can't hurt me anymore.

◆ Getting gifts on my birthday and Christmas are important to me. And when I say "a gift," I don't mean a pool table or tickets to a fishing tournament.

◆ Your unwillingness to help me makes me feel like you don't care about me.

◆ I'm not feeling well, and I need you to take on some extra responsibilites while I rest.

Do we assume that men should know all about what we feel, what we think and what we need? A wise woman will inform her man. She will prime his old, rusty communication pump by letting him know that she needs to be listened to and responded to verbally.

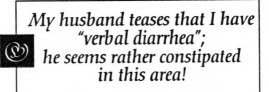

> *My husband teases that I have "verbal diarrhea"; he seems rather constipated in this area!*

The stereotype of the chatterbox wife who talks, complains, and nags so constantly that her husband deafens himself to everything she says, is all too familiar. It's almost as common as the one about the philandering husband who tells one sympathetic female admirer after the next: "My wife just doesn't understand me..." In actuality, the wife probably understands her husband far too well, despite the fact that he hasn't talked to her for twenty-five years!

Beloved writer Jamie Buckingham made an interesting observation. He wrote that God gave Adam the command not to eat of the tree long before Eve was even created! Therefore the whole problem with the human race is caused by one root thing:

> ## Eden's biggest problem? Adam didn't talk to his woman!

Adam knew everything God wanted, but he just didn't communicate it to his wife. Then he was too busy "dressing the garden." When he wouldn't talk to her she finally wandered off and found some slick fellow who *would* talk to her!

LOOK WHO'S TALKING!

Stereotypes aside, wherever men and women are together, there are, to say the least, occasional problems in communication. And, even among researchers and therapists, there are both agreements and disagreements about the ins and outs of male-female conversation.

Gary Smalley, a well-known Christian family counselor, states that women use twice as many words a day as men, a claim he asserts is confirmed by researchers. His assessment of women's "doubletalk" is based on his belief that men are more concerned with information than women, who are more concerned with emotions. He remarks in *Hidden Keys to Loving Relationships*, "When the average male runs out of facts, he'll stop talking."[1]

From a different perspective, Deborah Tannen in her best-selling book *You Just Don't Understand*, reports that during seven university faculty meetings, "men spoke more often and, without exception, spoke for a longer time. The men's turns ranged from 10.66 to 17.07 seconds, while the women's turns ranged from 3 to 10 seconds. In other words, the women's longest turns were still shorter than the men's shortest turns."

Her conclusion is that, in public, men do far more talking. However, in private conversation, she agrees that women are more talkative. Tannen says, "Another way of capturing these differences is by using the terms *report-talk* and *rapport-talk.*"[2]

Both Tannen and Smalley agree that women are seeking to connect, while their men are more concerned with the exchange of information. This conclusion is reached by countless other therapists, researchers and observers. Most experts deduce:

> *Men talk to share facts.*
> *Women talk to*
> *share feelings.*

Communication is a double-edged sword. Not only is it a battleground in its own right, it is also an essential place for resolving other conflicts. If we can learn the essentials of good communication, we'll have an extra measure of peace in our most important relationships.

Probably the biggest land mines hidden in the communications battlefield are these:

◆ Fear of communication
◆ Inability to listen

- Always talking about negatives
- Personal attacks
- Dishonesty
- Needing to be right
- Poor timing
- Repetition (Nagging)
- Walking out

ARE YOU AFRAID TO COMMUNICATE?

Kathy was anything but a nagging female. She grew up in a family that argued constantly–her parents bickered, her brothers and sisters punched each other, and dinner time was sometimes reduced to food fights. A quiet, thoughtful child, Kathy rarely participated in the conflicts. She listened, however, and made a promise to herself before she reached her teens: "When I'm grown up, I am never going to argue with anyone."

Kathy became the kind of adult female who tries to make everything all right. She never expressed negative feelings to anyone. Instead, she put on a big smile and complied with whatever anyone asked of her. When she met Ray, she was swept off her feet. Realizing how much she loved him, she made an even greater commitment never to mar their sweet love with disagreeable words.

Unfortunately, although Ray loved Kathy deeply, he was a very domineering kind of guy. And since Kathy set no boundaries for him, he walked all over her. He molded her into "my little lady." Eventually Kathy woke up and decided she was tired of being "little-lady-like." But by the time she rebelled against Ray's total control over her, it was almost too late.

Her fear of communication all but destroyed a potentially rewarding relationship. She was living out the Bible proverb: "The fear of man lays a snare" (Proverbs 29:25).

People fear communication because of:

◆ Avoidance of conflict
◆ Weak communication skills
◆ Fear of criticism
◆ Past abuse
◆ Uncertainty about issues
◆ Desire to appear compliant
◆ Hidden agendas
◆ Fear of loss

These are *not* good reasons to evade conversation. However, it's wise to remember that a quiet, pensive man or woman-of-few-words may not fear communication at all. He (or she) may simply find too much talk tedious and unnecessary.

Personality differences have a great deal to do with whether or not conversations ever get started or last more than thirty seconds. If the "opposites attract" principle has matched you up with a noncommunicator, you may be faced with one of those unchangeable facts of life. Rather than struggling to change your partner, you may simply need to accept his or her golden silence with a measure of serene acceptance.

ARE YOU LISTENING TO ME?

The cartoon character George, hidden behind his newspaper, is a classic illustration of a man who is not listening. Even when they aren't escaping behind reading materials, both men and women sometimes have a hard time quieting their own racing thoughts long enough to really hear what is being said to them. Sometimes we're more interested in finishing other people's sentences for them than hearing them out.

It should be obvious to anyone who longs for conversation that listening is just as important as speaking. Of course this can be a bit challenging to some of our more self-centered friends.

After bragging and posturing about his successes for about an hour, generous Jason said to his date, "Hey, we've talked about me enough! Now let's talk about you. What do *you* think of me?"

New ways of listening. Beyond our actual *hearing* of words and our initial response to their meaning, we men and women have to learn new ways of listening to each other.

Dr. John Gray, in *Men Are from Mars, Women Are from Venus*, observes that even when men listen to a woman, they sometimes hear something quite different from what the woman means. He says,

> The number one complaint women have in relationships is: "I don't feel heard." Even this complaint is misunderstood by men. A man's literal translation of "I don't feel heard" leads him to invalidate and argue with her feelings. He thinks he has heard her if he can repeat what she has said. A (better) translation of a woman saying "I don't feel heard" is: "I feel as though you don't fully understand what I really mean to say or care about how I feel. Would you show me that you are interested in what I have to say?"[3]

Boldly stated, she is saying, "Do you hear me? Do you care how I feel? Do you understand? Are you interested?"

Defensiveness distorts meaning. On the other hand, men often feel accused and criticized by women's more or less innocent comments. Here are some examples:

She says	She means	He hears
I don't have a thing to wear.	Help me decide.	Buy me more clothes.
I'm exhausted.	Let's relax together.	You don't work as hard as I do.

Sex isn't as exciting as it used to be.	*Let's experiment.*	*You're a lousy lover.*
Fine!	*Forget it! I'm frustrated...*	*You're too stupid to understand me.*
I dread Christmas.	*I need your help.*	*You always ruin Christmas.*
We're always rushing.	*Life is hectic.*	*You're always late.*
I'm bored.	*I need a change of scenery.*	*You're boring.*

If we know at the outset that men and women use language differently, we can save ourselves a measure of misunderstanding.

> **Women**—communicate more clearly what you want. **Men**—listen less defensively, from the heart, not the head.

Touchy subjects. There are four major problem topics on which a husband and wife must learn to communicate. These areas often wind up being the battlegrounds which lead to marital discord and sometimes even divorce:

123

1. Sex
2. Finances
3. In-laws
4. Kids

It stands to reason that our communication must frequently address these loaded issues, even though at times they are the very last things we want to talk about. Since they are so dangerous, they must be handled with love and understanding. Our communication skills have to be developed and honed, so that differences can be settled early and equitably.

WATCH YOUR TONE OF VOICE!

I am fascinated with different languages, and I've learned how *different meanings* can be attached to identical words. I speak a little Chinese (Mandarin), but I have gotten myself into trouble practicing my language on people who speak it fluently.

In this enchanting language, there are five levels of intonation for the same written characters. Thus the sing-song, almost musical sound English-speakers identify in Chinese speech. The slightest incorrect intonation on a word can totally alter its meaning.

This isn't true only in Chinese. Intonation can also play havoc with male-female dialogues in English. For example, if one of you says "OK" it can mean,

"I understand."

"I agree."

"Yeah, I hear you talking."

"Stop bugging me."

"No way do I buy that one!"

(Pause in your reading for a moment. Become a play-actor and practice all the different nuances that you can convey in your "OK"!)

WORDS FOR THE WISE

No matter what it is we're talking about, the fine art of listening is a skill worth developing for all of us. Here are a few important points:

◆ Look into the speaker's eyes.

◆ Nod, smile, frown or otherwise respond to what's being said.

◆ Try to "hear" not only the words, but the emotions behind the words.

◆ Don't look at your watch, scan the room for more interesting companions, or turn on the television.

◆ Don't interrupt.

◆ Wait until the speaker has finished articulating his or her complete thought before you answer.

WHY, YOU DIRTY SO-AND-SO!

Most communication is simply a sharing of ideas, but from time to time, disagreement and conflict are involved in the exchange. One of the most damaging aspects of verbal dispute is the bad habit some of us have of simply *attacking the person* rather than *addressing the issue*.

"Sticks and stones may break my bones but words can never harm me" is a familiar playground response to insults. But it's not true. Words can harm us very much. It is a known fact that harsh words are just as damaging to the soul as physical blows. Harsh, accusatory words teach our partners that it is not safe to talk to us.

It should be a law:

 Insults are illegal in healthy communication.

A word to the wise—sarcastic humor and "teasing" may be masked putdowns. Psychologists call this "passive-aggressive behavior." That means that, rather than directly attacking, we do it in a hidden way. Masked or not, insults are inappropriate when we're seriously trying to communicate.

WHY DON'T YOU JUST TELL THE TRUTH?

Just as there are many subtle ways of being insulting, there are many kinds of lies. Some people are very careful about the words they say, but they lie in gestures, innu-endoes, implications and in other ways. Later on, with innocent faces, they say "I've never lied to you!"

Other people believe with all their hearts that they are

telling the truth, but they are lying to themselves. The importance of truth-telling in good communication should be obvious, but getting at the truth may be more difficult than we realize. It requires personal accountability as well as simple honesty.

Trish was feeling very blue. All in the same day she had been reprimanded by her boss, had discovered that her rent was being raised, and had received a notice from the local college that her application was rejected. To make things worse, there was her PMS, which she had scarcely factored into the situation.

What justifies my existence? she thought. *And what can make me feel better right now?* She wanted and needed some encouragement, affirmation, even direction for her future.

She knew that Ron, her boyfriend, was a man of few words. In fact, he rarely came up with any loving compliments on his own, let alone deep reflections. *He* never worried about his philosophy of life. "I am a twenty-two-year-old pharmacy student named Ron, from Cleveland" would have been an adequate life-justifying statement for Ron.

The thing Ron *could* talk about was wanting Trish as his fiancée. They had known each other for almost two years, and for most of the past six months, he had been asking her for a commitment.

She liked him well enough, probably even loved him, but she just wasn't quite sure....

"Ron, it's me," she said on the phone, her voice flat.

"Trishie, Hi. How's it going?"

"OK, I guess. Listen, I think I've made up my mind. Do

you finally want to spend some money on a ring?"

"Are you kidding?! Of course I do! I knew you'd say yes eventually! When can I see you?..."

Jeweler's box in hand, Ron was at her door a few days later.

"Hi, Ron..." This time Trish's voice was flat for a different reason. She was no longer suffering from PMS and her job was going better. But she had spent the several days mulling over her precipitous move. *What have I done? I'm as good as engaged already! And I'm still not so sure about it. What made me do that?*

"I did it, Trish! Here it is! When we get inside, I'll slip it onto your finger... Hey, what's going on? Aren't you glad to see me?..."

"Uh... Ron... I've been thinking it over."

> *Before couples attempt to communicate, the first thing they have to do is explore their own hearts and seek the truth within themselves.*

Another relationship hits a land mine. Maybe they'll be able to regroup and go on. Maybe not. Trish and Ron's story happens to illustrate many of the male-female issues I have been describing throughout this book.

But the most glaring fault here is Trish's lack of honesty.

Sure, she was depressed. Granted that distorts a woman's

reasoning. But fundamentally, she was dishonest, first with herself and then with Ron. When all she needed were a few kind words, a little affirmation, she tried to pull Ron's strings with the one subject guaranteed to please him.

She could have asked Ron for affirmation or advice. Even Ron-of-few-words could have obliged, especially with her coaching.

The warmth she really needed wasn't even forthcoming when she gave him the big "Yes" he had been waiting for. Honest expression of need, even if it's from a state of confusion, is what works. Dishonesty backfires. It's manipulative. It's a land mine.

Before couples attempt to communicate, the first thing they have to do is explore their own hearts and seek the truth within themselves. This isn't easy. We read King David's prayers in his psalms, "Search me, O God, and know my heart!... Put false ways far from me" (Psalms 139:23; 119:29).

Passionate man that he was, David was well aware that his deepest motivations were sometimes hidden, even from himself. (Reread the Bathsheba story, recounted in 2 Samuel 11.) We are all well-advised to do some soul-searching before we launch into serious dialogue with our partners. Besides, they may know us better than we think.

Honesty has another aspect, too. It *does* mean truthfulness. It *doesn't* mean telling every aspect of the truth, in every circumstance, to every person. If we are truly instructed to "love your neighbor as you love yourself," surely we are to give the same consideration toward sensitivity and kindness that we would want to receive. "Speaking the truth *in love*" is a powerful concept when combined with wisdom and discretion, grace and forgiveness.

One reason honesty is so important in communication is because our lies have a way of coming back to haunt us. They will eventually discredit us and cause our partners to lose faith. At the very least, they will prevent us from having the kind of open, forthright relationships we want and need.

I'M RIGHT, SO DON'T CONFUSE ME WITH FACTS!

There are people, both male and female, who always find winning more important than loving. This may have to do with insecurity (which is nothing but pride in disguise), personality, family background, or just being ticked off. Having to be right, no matter what, is an unattractive attribute, but even the best of us fall into its trap from time to time.

◆ Sometimes we want the other person to admit he's wrong for once.

◆ Sometimes we want to punish our antagonist by humiliating him.

◆ Sometimes we are determined to prove a point because we know beyond a doubt that it's true.

◆ Sometimes we think we're dealing with an eternal or spiritual value, and we feel we can't ethically give up unless we win.

◆ Sometimes we want to avoid looking foolish to those who are listening.

◆ Sometimes our area of expertise is being threatened, and it makes us feel defensive.

◆ Sometimes we are loyally defending another person, and want to win on their behalf.

◆ Sometimes we are too angry to stop fighting.

◆ Sometimes we enjoy the stimulation of the battle itself.

◆ Sometimes we are tired of losing.

Whatever the motivation to keep fighting, it's worth remembering that *people are more important than issues.*

YOUR ATTENTION, PLEASE

Knowing how to communicate involves knowing when you've communicated enough; understanding when it's time to stop. Timing is everything, and that brings us back to an important point: men's compartmentalized thinking.

A woman can talk on the phone while working at the kitchen sink. She can make a grocery list while watching *Oprah.* Once we accept the fact that a man is wired differently, and finds it difficult to respond to more than one stimulus at a time, we'll wait for a time when he can absorb what we say and can respond properly. The following principle will require great patience when applied to some men, and will prove virtually impossible to follow when applied to others. However, it's worth considering: *She* should wait to communicate until nothing else has *his* attention.

If I've told you once, I've told you a thousand times. In another chapter, we'll take a look at the reasons women nag. And, by the way, that's not to say that men can't be nags, too, although women seem to enjoy a certain reputation in that regard. But ceaseless repetition of certain facts, feelings, or instructions means certain death to constructive communication.

In a survey of children's primary complaints with their parents, repeated reminders scored high at the top of their "this really bugs me" inventory. Sometimes we think that we aren't really nagging. We're just reviewing certain past failures or frustrations to underscore their significance. Or we're concerned that our voice may not have been heard the last thirty-eight times we said the same thing. Or we're practicing the "broken record" technique of conversation.

Enough, already!

The only words worth repeating daily are "I love you" and "I'm sorry." Our childrearing and our success in marriage will improve if we try to remove old tapes from our stock of responses. For one thing, our requests, corrections and complaints will more likely be heard if they're not the same worn-out words. For another, we've probably got lots of new ammo by now anyway!

CAN WE TALK?

Bear in mind that, when you do make time for conversation, the subject shouldn't always be a negative one. We can't always be peering over our glasses mumbling, "We've got to talk." Let's be sure we punctuate our communication times with some positive, enjoyable talks.

Be unpredictable in your communication sessions; have something interesting or stimulating to say. Share a story or an enjoyable experience of the day. If every time we say "I need to talk to you," it's bomb-dropping time, our partner will learn to begin to cringe.

If you do have a problem to solve, let your man know that it's not a big thing, but it is important to you. Plan on being Iron Jane with a mission to accomplish, not Rambling Rose, who rambles on and gets nowhere with her tangents. That kind of conversation prompts the male comments: "OK, but cut to the chase. C'mon! What's the bottom line?"

I can relate to this because as I said earlier, my husband says I often suffer from "verbal diarrhea" while I feel he is a bit "constipated" in the communication area. We're working on it together.

THAT'S IT! I'M OUT OF HERE…

Most of us have heard of the "fight or flight" response to danger. And it doesn't appear that either men or women have the monopoly on it. Fight or flight seems to have more to do with personality than gender, and we all have our favorite techniques for dealing with unpleasantness.

In their book *The Power of Love,* David and Janet Congo list four principles for dealing with conflict. They are:

Yield............................your way
Win................................my way
Resolve ....our way
Withdraw.....................no way

They discuss the withdrawal (or walking out, flight-response) to conflict like this,

> Remember, the opposite of love is not hate; it is indifference. If you are married to someone who withdraws, you know what indifference feels like. The withdrawer removes himself or herself not only from the conflict, but from the relationship as well.... The person who walks away from conflict disconnects emotionally from hurt while hurting the other with indifference. Distance is stretched between the two, and any hope of resolution is dashed."[4]

Finding our way onto the communication battlefield without tripping land mines is vital. It begins with an awareness of our inherent differences in communicating. In general (and as always there are notable exceptions) when it comes to conversation...

Men *compete.*
Women *connect.*
Men seek *independence.*
Women seek *interaction.*

> Men focus on the *outer* world.
> Women focus on the *inner* world.
>
> Men speak of *facts*.
> Women speak of *feelings*.
>
> Men listen *defensively*.
> Women listen *emotionally*.

What is Iron Jane to do, when confronted with this very strategic battlefield called communication? Besides arming herself with truth, self-respect, and determination to both speak and listen, she is going to have to make sure that love is her first priority. Her sensitivity will protect and nurture her most precious relationships. The steel in her soul will provide determination, honesty, and perseverance. It will open up transformative dialogue about difficult issues, so she won't just turn tail and run like a coward. It will enable her to embrace and enjoy the man in her life without losing herself in the process.

> *Maturity is knowing the*
> *difference between what*
> *makes him tick, and*
> *what makes him ticked!*

Chapter 8

The Testosterone Syndrome

It was Kate's birthday, and she and her husband Brett were sitting happily by the fireplace while she opened presents. She had received several gifts from her parents, brothers, and sisters, as well as a couple of friends. Once they had been opened and examined she looked at Brett expectantly. Looking a bit sheepish, he pulled a small package out of his pocket.

Since it was his only gift to her, Kate imagined that it would be something rather special. She studied the soft parcel, trying to guess, her eyes bright with anticipation.

After tearing off the paper, her expression was puzzled. She found herself examining an unfamiliar apparel item; for some reason she was now the proud possessor of a tiny black lace G-string with a strategically placed red heart on the front.

"It's... it's... certainly small, isn't it?" Unsure whether Brett was joking or serious, she studied his face.

Brett grinned broadly. "It's just a little reminder that I love you."

Kate was more puzzled than ever. "I know you love me, Brett. But I've never worn a G-string in my life."

"Well, it's really part of the bigger present I'm giving you."

Much relieved, Kate ventured, "Oh, really?" She scanned the room. "Where is it?" she inquired.

"You're looking at it, Babe!" Brett exclaimed, pulling her into a rather aggressive embrace, and then laying her down on the floor next to him. "It's me! I'm your present! You've been wanting a baby, right? And you said you wanted a birthday present that would always remind you of me, right? So—starting tonight, we're going to make a baby. Of course the G-string's going to help us get started!"

Kate stared at Brett in disbelief. He had to be kidding. Didn't he? He was joking. Wasn't he?

Brett's face was a portrait of glee. Obviously quite satisfied with his presentation, he continued to make certain relevant moves. It didn't seem likely that he would suddenly sit up and say, "OK, it was just a joke. Here are your diamond earrings, Kate."

No, Brett wasn't kidding. He was much deflated when

Kate began to weep, ran upstairs and called her mother. He scratched his head, trying to understand.

Meanwhile, Kate was listening to her mother's familiar and disgusted voice saying, "Well, I'll be! If that isn't just like a man!"

MAJOR CONFLICT OF INTEREST

Now, simply to agree with Kate's mother would be unfair to most men. It really isn't "just like a man" for a man to offer himself sexually as a birthday present. In fact, it's pretty unusual. However, Brett's birthday gift bomb does illustrate quite vividly an ever-present problem between males and females.

> ### *Sex both brings us together and keeps us apart.*

Most men feel that their sex lives are OK—an "eight" on a scale of one to ten. Many of their wives will shake their heads at the same question, and when asked they'll say, "Oh, it's about a two." Men often feel that women are sexually unresponsive. Women often feel that men are sexually obsessed. There are complex reasons for these differences.

This chapter, of course, is not intended to be a sex manual. If that's the kind of help you need, all sorts of excellent books are available. But sexuality differs greatly between males and females, and it's important for us to explore what makes us alike and what makes us different.

Men, in a general sense, equate their entire being to their sexuality. Women are not so consciously sexual, and sometimes even deny their sexuality in efforts to appear spiritual or "ladylike."

Because of both hormones and anatomy, men struggle with sexual urges and vulnerability to a degree that few women understand. (If they did, there might be fewer mini-skirts and skin-tight tank tops in the workplace!)

> *"Sex appeal is 50 percent what you've got, and 50 percent what people think you've got."*
> –Actress Sophia Loren

In his landmark book *The Sexual Man,* Dr. Archibald Hart, Dean of Fuller Seminary's Graduate School of Psychology, makes this rather startling statement:

Sure, the average man occasionally thinks of other things like football and politics, but eventually all mental roads lead back to this one central fixation: Sex. There are times when the obsession fades and even vanishes. Not many times, but there are some times. Give him an intense challenge at work. Let him buy a new computer or sports car. Give him a golf bag or a fishing trip. He'll forget about sex for a while. Sooner or later, like a smoldering fire, it will flare up again. Strong, urgent, forceful and impatient, the sex drive dominates the mind and body of every healthy male. Like it or not that's the way it is.[1]

Dr. Hart goes on to say that many good, normal men feel shame about their sexuality, and that many women are utterly unaware of this aspect of male mentality. There seems to be a great, silent gulf between men and women when sexual understanding is sought. Because of cultural, religious and family stigmas, it is difficult for many couples to overcome their self-consciousness and to become vulnerable and forthright with each other about their needs, wants and feelings.

Malcolm Muggeridge is quoted as having said, "It must be admitted that we English have sex on the brain, which is a very unfortunate place to have it." English men may well have sex on the brain, but I don't think that means they understand their drives any better.

Most men in the Western world have their sexuality wrapped up in their self-esteem. Women are aware that men have sensitive egos when it comes to sex. You may have heard comments like, "Reject him sexually and you've rejected his whole being, as far as he's concerned." Wives quickly learn that to say, "No, not tonight," may even bring forth some subtle form of retaliation in following days. In some cases, it may be less than subtle.

Geoff took Amanda in his arms, kissing her good night in her living room. He didn't want to leave–the candles were still burning, the music was still playing, and he was feeling quite unsatisfied. Thus far, the two had never made love, and Amanda was determined that they wouldn't unless they were married. Geoff agreed with her in principle, but couldn't have cared less about principles at that particular romantic moment.

Softly, sweetly, he pulled Amanda down next to him on the couch. His hands began to move in new directions. Amanda stiffened. After a few moments, she pushed him away gently and stood up. "I... I think you'd better go... it's getting late," she murmured.

"Just a minute longer, Sweetheart. You know I love you."

"I love you, too," she nodded, surprised to hear him saying those "three little words." He'd never told her that before. Maybe...

He drew her against him again. She tenderly kissed his cheek, shook her head and smiled. "You're tempting me. No, you'd better go."

Geoff left, as good-naturedly as possible. But he was frustrated, not only sexually but emotionally. He felt rejected and deflated. Even though he knew very well that Amanda was right in her response, he resented it. If she really loved him, why wouldn't she want to make love to him? Was she ambivalent, or was he? He felt confused and annoyed.

The next morning, when he picked her up for church, Geoff was still quiet and moody. At lunch he casually began to tell Amanda about two other girls at work who were interested in him. After feeling warm and close to him because he'd finally said "I love you," she now felt chilled and devastated. What was she to make of his veiled threats that someone else might love him just a bit more than she did? What on earth was going on with Geoff's affections?

Of course Geoff was retaliating after Amanda's refusal to give him her all. He somehow suspected that her turn-down was more than it appeared to be. In spite of his own morals and basically respectable value system, he still viscerally felt somehow unloved and undesirable. His self-esteem was more tightly connected to his sexuality than he realized.

> *Men often feel that women are sexually unresponsive. Women often feel that men are sexually obsessed.*

By and large, partly because men–especially godly, religious men–don't talk about it openly, and partly because women have such a difficult time relating to it, females don't have a clue about the way men feel, think, respond, react, and struggle sexually. And men cannot comprehend women's cyclical sexual interest, which comes and goes like the tide.

As far as a man's concerned, he's ready, willing, and able to make love at the drop of a suggestive smile. As for her? "I want a lover with a slow hand" isn't just a Pointer Sisters' song. It's a cry for help!

> One husband remarked, "I can't
> remember the last time we had
> sex." His wife glared at him.
> "Well I can, and that's why
> we're not doing it any more."

MAKING LOVE SHOULD BE A FINE ART

Besides having feelings of being on the receiving end of their man's boundless sexual energy, many women are offended by the lack of skill their men demonstrate in the process of making love.

As actress Glenda Jackson remarked, "The important thing in acting is being able to laugh and cry. If I have to laugh, I think of my sex life. If I have to cry, I think of my sex life."

Another woman commented, "The last time my husband made love to me, it lasted one hour and ten minutes... but that was the night we turned our clocks back."

That last statement probably summarizes one of the biggest complaints women have about sex, besides having to perform whether they feel like it or not. It is difficult for men to understand that women want to be led to a point of love-making through a process of affection, romance and endearment. It could take all night, as far as many females are concerned, and that would be wonderful.

Meanwhile, the man, who has caught a glimpse of his woman's breast or a thigh, is completely prepared to begin and end the sexual event during half time on Monday Night Football.

Dr. James Dobson comments on this disparity in his book, *What Wives Wish Their Husbands Knew about Women,*

First, men are primarily excited by visual stimulation. They are turned on by feminine nudity or peek-a-boo glimpses of semi-nudity.... Women, by contrast, are much less visually oriented than men. Sure they are interested in attractive masculine bodies, but the physiological mechanism of sex is not triggered typically by what they see; woman are stimulated primarily by the sense of touch."[2]

After talking to hundreds of women, I would add the *sense of hearing* (I love you, you're beautiful), the *sense of awareness* (he's been trying to help around the house; he's made a big effort to listen to me), and the *sense of smell* (he's finally bought an antiperspirant; he stopped using that disgusting dimestore aftershave!).

Of course, there's no debate about a man's primary sex organ. Everyone knows about that. But it has been said that a woman's primary sex organ is somewhat different. It is *her brain* (whether she's English or not!).

DON'T WANT TO TALK ABOUT IT

In actual fact, it is very difficult for some women to discuss their sexuality with men. First of all, many women want to say things like "Hold me.... Talk to me.... Write me love letters.... Bring me flowers." Unfortunately, it often comes out sounding like, "Can't you even hug me one time without touching me *there?*"

Most men eventually learn to reach out to women with affection before they make a power move. And many women will respond to their man's direct sexual overtures in the hope of being held and embraced in the process.

To oversimplify the male-female sexual dilemma, it might look something like this:

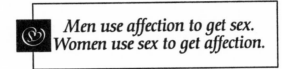

> *Men use affection to get sex.*
> *Women use sex to get affection.*

Men have to be educated about women's need for affection. They not only have to understand it, they also have to be willing to respect it. And women need to know that it isn't the most natural thing in the world for most males to simply sit and hold their women without any overt sexual gestures.

Once they have found their way into the bedroom, most men don't know instinctively what gives pleasure to their partners. Matters are further complicated because some women, particularly those with conservative religious backgrounds, find it difficult to initiate sex, to talk about their sexual desires and wishes, or to respond unselfconsciously when they are excited.

A couple tried to talk about the delicate matter of improving their love life. "Honey," Bev said, "We have a problem...."

"Not again," Ed grunted.

"Well, it's our sex life. I'm not really satisfied. My needs just aren't being met."

146

"Great! So you want *more?*"

"No, you don't understand. I'm looking for quality, not quantity."

Ed responded typically, "OK. So what am I doing wrong?"

"It's not a matter of right and wrong. It's about us giving pleasure to each other."

Ed glanced at the television. "Do we have to talk about this now?"

"When *are* we going to talk about it? I guess maybe I'll just talk to someone else. How about Dave, next door? Dave knows a lot about sex. Or maybe Pastor Bob? I could call…"

"OK, OK. What do you want to talk about?"

GOD ISN'T STRAIT-LACED ABOUT SEX

In actual fact, God is no prude. There are different parts of the human sexuality system that he created *solely* for our pleasure; they are not necessary for procreation.

Sex appears in the Bible in more places than I can count. And it's not just "Jesse begat David; David begat Solomon," etc.! The Bible very clearly endorses sexual pleasure and human sexual passion. If you don't believe me, read Song of Solomon, which is one of the most erotic literary works ever written.

Of course there are godly controls as to "with whom" we should make love. But no biblical guidelines or limitations exist regarding the "how-tos." The "whom" is clearly limited to a spouse (of the opposite sex, by the way!). But you won't find verses commanding the man to make the first move, or the woman to comply, headache or not.

Scripture simply presumes that males and females will experience lusty sexuality—that's the way God made us.

SEXUAL BLACKMAIL

One of the most familiar accusations men make against women is that women use sex as a weapon, or as a means of manipulation. And this isn't a totally unfair assertion, although women may not see what they are doing as clearly as they might.

Just because I'm not in the mood doesn't automatically hoist an inner red flag which says, "No sex." After all, would I not give my husband supper, just because I had no appetite? I can be in control of changing my mood, of communicating my feelings, and of making adjustments to my expectations, all without sacrificing who I am.

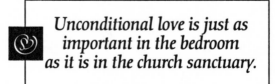

> *Unconditional love is just as important in the bedroom as it is in the church sanctuary.*

Even more importantly, using sex as a way of "teaching him a lesson" or of saying "I don't feel like making love to you because you aren't making me happy" is another form of manipulative, conditional love.

Unconditional love is just as important in the bedroom as it is in the church sanctuary. We all need to be loved

unconditionally, and we need to love others unconditionally, particularly when things aren't going so well
between us.

SOME SEXUAL NO-NOES

What are other areas in which sex becomes a problem
between men and women?

◆ Some women give sex to their husbands only because
they are married and *they are obligated to*. They may be
unable to achieve orgasm. They may have built up
resentments that cause them to be unresponsive. Or
they have false guilt about sexual enjoyment. In a very
real sense, these women are simply "servicing" their
mates, creating a loveless and joyless bedroom experience. I call this the "dead birdie" act.

◆ Some men seek sex because they have developed an
obsession with it, either because of feelings of insecurity,
or because they are driven by uncontrolled chemical
urges in their bodies. They may be reinforcing their masculinity or they may be seeking an outlet for tension and
anxiety, using the sexual act as a "tranquilizer." Such a
man may want to have sex every day, or even several
times a day, without concern for his wife's feelings.

◆ Some couples use sex *in place of verbal communication*, trying to gloss over their problems with powerful sexual
responses. Sex is a form of communication, but it is no
substitute for open, frank dialogue and forthright
problem-solving.

◆ In another form of manipulation, some wives provide *sex as a reward* for their husbands' good behavior. This woman may decide to make love to her spouse after he's taken her shopping, or after he's received a large commission check, or after he's cleaned out the garage.

◆ There are men whose machismo requires them to conquer their women every few days. It is not an act of love that drives them into the bedroom, but *an act of aggressive pursuit and conquest.* These men usually have to hear more than "a word to the wise" before they are able to get the picture.

◆ In unmarried couples particularly, women use sex in an attempt *to secure a commitment* from a man, or to entice him into a more affectionate relationship. There are probably more tears shed by single women over this particular mistake than over any other. Women who try this tactic almost universally end up feeling used and abandoned.

◆ Unmarried men sometimes move from one sexual partner to the next simply to satisfy a craving for gratification *without emotional entanglement.* They may find it necessary to brag to their male friends about their exploits, or they may be more secretive about their activities, determined to make every woman they meet feel like "the only one."

WHERE'S THE ROMANCE?

Practically every book that's ever been written about sexual issues reminds men that women need to be romanced, no matter how long they've been married. Perhaps this is more easily said than done, after years of sharing bathrooms and needing mouthwash in the morning. (In medieval times, before mouthwash, a woman could divorce a man for having bad breath!)

Fortunately, it is possible to keep the flame alive, if efforts are made by both partners. Mutual romance requires sensitivity, generosity of spirit, openness of heart, and a good, hefty measure of creativity and imagination. And it requires caution against outside distractions.

In our media-driven world, it's easy to wander off on sweet fantasy trips that make our day-to-day reality seem tame. Too many sensuous novels, too many wildly provocative movies, too many amorous love songs–all these can make us begin to compare a comfortable, sometimes rather dull, mate with some exciting dream lover.

How many marriages have been permanently damaged by adulterous affairs that started as "innocent daydreams"? A woman becomes bored, disenchanted and critical. She "miraculously" meets some man who seems like the one she's been waiting for all her life, the one who understands, the one who truly cares. She starts flirting with him, having lunch with him, working on projects with him, telling her troubles to him. Her husband and the years she has invested in her relationship with him are instantly eclipsed by a fantasy.

That fantasy may well turn into a sexual encounter, an affair, and ultimately a marital tragedy. These things happen more quickly, and more often, than any of us would care to think. May God help us to guard our hearts, our bodies, and our marriages! Let's make the most of what we've got.

MRS. IRON JANE

One of Iron Jane's most important traits is her courage to openly discuss difficult subjects. Overcoming fears and hang-ups, being assertive enough to say, "This is what I like!", and finding the right time and place for the conversation is a challenging assignment. Strong on the inside, sensitive on the outside–that's the secret to Iron's Jane's success, and in no place is it more important than on the sexual "battlefield."

The fact is, no woman should be ashamed of her sexuality. Feelings of pleasure and well-being are part of our heritage from our Creator. It's up to us, however, to communicate openly and clearly with our mates so that we aren't hiding aspects of ourselves or expecting them to read our minds.

Can it be done? Let's choose a metaphor. Like a delicate flower, the romance between a man and woman must be carefully tended. Surrounding weeds of resentment and bitterness must be pulled up by their roots. The water of selfless love must be generously showered upon it. The sunlight of affection must shine regularly, brightly, and without a shadow of regret or retaliation. And the nurturing provided by open and honest conversation is the final step necessary to keep the romance flower alive, budding and blooming for a lifetime.

Or, if we likened our sexual experience to playing tennis, we could say to ourselves:

◆ This is my permanent tennis partner.

◆ I will not have another partner to play with.

◆ I will not look for an alternate.

◆ I will not even think about playing tennis with another partner.

◆ We could go together for tennis lessons.

◆ I will not walk off the court; I'll improve my serve!

Is it possible for men and women to achieve sexual understanding with each other? Yes, if we are willing to communicate, accept, forgive, laugh, experiment, express ourselves, enjoy, and celebrate. Let's put it this way–men and women will never be identical, but we can have a lifetime of pleasure exploring and discovering our unique and fascinating differences.

> *"There may be some things better than sex, and there may be some things worse. But there's nothing exactly like it."*
> –W.C. Fields, Actor

Chapter 9

In the Spirit
of True Love

As I hauled my packages into the mall parking lot, the location of my car was a bit vague in my memory. While visiting two dozen stores and handing over more money than I could believe, my car's very existence had seemed insignificant. Now I wished I'd paid closer attention. I did remember one important fact, however: it was parked next to a beautiful red Jaguar.

Around and around I plodded, carrying my burden of parcels, searching desperately for a glimpse of elegant red paint. Finally, by sheer coincidence, I tripped over my car.

The red Jag was no longer parked next to it; therefore I had lost my way.

It occurred to me that this is a good example of our world's view of spirituality–it is based on ever-changing standards; there are no absolutes, no fixed truths, no unchanging values. Our modern world moves moral landmarks around the way the red Jaguar was moved– one minute they are there, the next minute they are gone.

> *Without immovable standards by which to measure our lives, we're all lost.*

STRENGTH THROUGH STANDARDS

What is true spirituality, anyway? Is it a New Age concept? Is it something we can learn from watching Oprah or a TV preacher? Is it simply a matter of getting in touch with our inner selves?

We know that spirituality is something more than keeping the Ten Commandments, and we know that these were not intended to be multiple choice options. But is true spirituality beyond us?

Maybe it's a matter of joining a particular church–*that's* the way to gain spiritual strength! Maybe the right one could transform a weak woman into an Iron Jane. Let's check out a few of them:

Presbyterians: God has predestined women to be strong.

Pentecostals: Spiritual gifts make a woman strong.

Positive Thinkers: Jane is strong because of her positive attitude.

Faith Thinkers: Jane needs to confess that she is strong.

Catholics: Church attendance makes Jane strong.

Baptists: When Jane is immersed, she'll come up strong.

The fact is, they are all correct and they all contribute to Jane's inner strength. But there's more to spirituality than any of that.

> *Some of us have been inoculated with small doses of Christianity, which keep us from catching the real thing.*

When we first considered Iron Jane and her place in the world, we agreed that she wasn't wearing a clanking, defensive suit of armor. But there are a couple of types of armor that are ideally suited to Jane. She's going to need them both.

First of all, the Bible says, "Let's put off the works of darkness and let us put on the armor of light" (Romans 13:12). It's interesting to think about the idea of putting "off the works of darkness."

PUTTING OFF THE WORKS OF DARKNESS

Whitney sat in my living room, telling me about her painful relationship with a man named Mike. She had been living with him for two years, and had just learned that he was using cocaine. He had also been somewhat abusive to her in recent weeks. Whitney's marriage had ended because of battering, and she saw the same thing happening again. She was feeling afraid.

"I really want you to pray for me, Lee," she said softly. "I know you believe in prayer, and I know prayer works."

"Of course I'll pray for you, Whitney. But you need to pray, too."

She smiled and shook her head. "I don't know how to pray, Lee."

"Prayer is just talking to God. It's not a big deal as far as how-tos are concerned."

"I guess it's pretty hard to believe that God would be interested in my problems, Lee. Besides, I haven't exactly lived a perfect life, if you know what I mean. I've broken some of the Ten Commandments."

I couldn't help but laugh. "Haven't we all? Listen, Whitney, there's one thing you need to understand right up front. Jesus Christ died on the cross so that you could pray to God without worrying about your sins. That's what being a Christian is all about–it's about knowing you're a sinner and accepting the fact that God paid for your sins with the life of his Son, Jesus."

"Well, of course I've heard about all that, but what's that got to do with praying about Mike?"

"It has everything to do with praying. Once you accept God's Son, Jesus, as the payment for your sins, and ask his Spirit to come into your heart, you will have free access to him with every problem, every need, every crisis you'll ever face."

"Do I need to ask God to forgive me before I pray?"

"You need to do it before you do another thing. You've already told me you're not perfect. So you agree that you're a sinner, right?"

"Right."

"OK, tell God what you've told me. Then ask him to forgive you and invite Jesus into your life. That's all you have to do. It's not that complicated—it's a simple surrender!"

Whitney sat quietly for a couple of minutes. Then she said, "God, I'm sorry I've sinned. Please forgive me, and please let Jesus come into my life. I need so much help and I don't know where else to turn."

She began to cry, and I prayed for her—not only for her salvation, but that God would show her his way of handling her problems with Mike.

Whitney called me bright and early the next morning. "I feel like a huge weight has been lifted off my heart, Lee. I've never felt such peace of mind."

Within two weeks, Whitney had found a roommate, broken off her relationship with Mike, moved out of his apartment, and started her life over. It wasn't easy—there were financial entanglements, emotional confrontations, and all kinds of begging and pleading from Mike.

But after a year and a half, Whitney was attending a Bible study, paying off her debts, dating a Christian man who adored her, and praying for others—including me!

> *Once you accept God's Son, Jesus, as the payment for our sins, and ask his Spirit to come into your heart, you will have free access to him with every problem, every need, every crisis you'll ever face.*

I still remember the night I surrendered my broken dreams to God. I was attending a Billy Graham Crusade as a teenager. I figured it was some kind of Holy Roller meeting and was curious to see what would happen there.

I was pleasantly surprised to discover quite a normal-looking crowd gathered to hear Dr. Graham's lecture. As I listened, I realized how nebulous my understanding of God really was. That night I surrendered my life to Jesus Christ, receiving him as my own Savior.

Without this spiritual infusion of power, I could never have made it through the rape and subsequent pregnancy that occurred just a year later. I tell this story in my book *The Missing Piece*. I have tested this "life in Christ" against some powerful odds and its validity has been proven to me again and again.

PUTTING ON THE ARMOR OF LIGHT

Putting off the works of darkness means trading in our old behavior for a new life of Jesus. Like Whitney, we have to acknowledge our sins, receive God's forgiveness through Christ's death and resurrection, and then ask him to guide us. We will then be wearing God's "armor of light."

Jesus Christ is the light of the world. When we choose to put on his armor of light, it means that we are walking in faith, hand-in-hand with our Savior.

This is an inner armor, not the visible callousness that too often characterizes the women of the 90s. The woman who wears the armor of light is vulnerable, loving and very much aware of who she is. (Without Jesus, she knows she is nothing.)

She is not kidding herself about her toughness or her frailties. But this doesn't mean that she volunteers herself to be a doormat to the world. Neither does she need to fight angrily against the unfair, "male-dominated" world she sees around her.

This woman sees life differently–by faith. She bathes herself in the light of the Scriptures. She prays daily to be forgiven, cleansed, helped, and protected in life's battles. She knows that she cannot successfully defend herself against all the things that can go wrong, but that she has a Defender who loves her fiercely, fights for her relentlessly, and stays at her side everlastingly.

Armor for spiritual battles. Her active combat is not against flesh and blood; she realizes that there are far worse forces at work in the world than male egos or testosterone! There are dangerous spiritual powers, driven by hate and destruction, constantly plotting against God's people–male and female alike. In fact, that's one primary

161

reason that bad things happen to good people.

It's because of those spiritual forces in the world that God has provided still another kind of armor. In the New Testament, Ephesians 6:13-17 describes "the whole armor of God." This kind of armor is intended to protect us in the midst of the spiritual warfare waged against us by the powers of darkness. Look it up and read the whole passage for yourself. We are to wear...

Righteousness as a strong breastplate to protect our hearts.

Peace as shoes to keep our feet on the right path.

Faith as a shield to deflect the darts and arrows of the enemy.

Salvation as a helmet to guard our minds against guilt, shame and fear.

Truth around our waists to hold us together in the midst of life's confusion.

God's Word, the Bible, to be our sword against all evil.

Spiritual—with or without a man. Some women feel that they are limited in their spiritual growth because their husbands refuse to take a role of spiritual leadership in the home. It's ideal for a man to take that role, but in reality few married women have husbands who boldly lead the family on spiritual adventures. This doesn't relegate such women to a kind of second-best Christianity. Not at all!

I can remember a time when I felt my spiritual growth was hampered because Hal didn't seem like he was "with the program." I felt that my own spiritual development was so tied into Hal's that mine was put on hold when he wasn't growing. I eventually learned that to God I am not "Mrs. Ezell"; I am "Lee," that same little girl he reached out for many years ago.

A walk with God is solitary. Whether we are single or married, we are responsible for our own relationship with the Lord. By relying on others, or worse yet by blaming them for not partnering with us, we miss the beautiful intimacy God wants to share with us, one on one, child and Heavenly Father.

WOUNDED WENDY

My friend Wendy was weakened by a difficult marriage and a subsequent divorce. When she described her husband's emotional abuse, which had gone on for years, it was evident that it had taken a terrible toll on her. I began to refer to him as "The Destroyer." This Terminator-type, destructive individual had convinced my friend that she was worthless and then had cruelly dumped her.

Although she was a faithful Christian, she was left wounded and feeble. Wendy felt doomed; she couldn't imagine having the strength to build a healthy relationship with a man.

Unfortunately, Wendy is not unlike many other women I talk to. Picking up the pieces after a failed relationship and trying to put life back together is a tough job. Such women need to be strengthened spiritually. They need to receive hope enough to risk again with a man, if that's God's will, and to be fortified with some wholesome principles.

Today Wendy talks joyfully about God's faithfulness. She's taken the time to "restore her soul" and has learned to walk with the Good Shepherd. Once she let go of "The Destroyer and the damage he'd done," I watched as the Lord brought a new man into her life. When he arrived, he found her to be both strong enough and receptive enough to build a beautiful relationship. They will be married soon.

Wounded Wendys can be transformed into Iron Janes by allowing the strength of God to be infused into their souls and by dressing in their spiritual armor. With that preparation, they are prepared to come to a new and helpful understanding of the differences that are built into the male psyche. This spiritually-empowered woman can begin to believe it is in fact possible to interact with a mate to the satisfaction of both parties—as impossible as that may have seemed to her before.

IRON JANE UNVEILED

Iron Jane chooses not to rage in frustration against the vast differences that exist between men and women. Instead, she accepts the fact that God has designed the sexes in a specific way for specific reasons. Her inner armor, the armor of God's pure light, makes her strong because she believes that he is able to make all things work together for her good (Romans 8:28).

She is equally convinced that God's plans for her are for good, not for calamity.

With this in mind, she is able to recycle some of the

garbage in her life. It's highly probable that some of the rubble may have piled up because of mistreatment by a male.

Jane is determined to fight off her bitterness and anger. She has learned that relying solely on a man—even a good, faithful man—is futile. She knows that only Jesus can be counted on to keep the lifetime promise: "I will never leave you or forsake you" (Hebrews 13:5).

She can laugh at "the time to come" (Proverbs 31:25) because her confidence buoys her good humor. The future, come what may, holds no terror for her because she has put her future in God's capable hands. This makes her stable emotionally, and able to grow spiritually.

She is increasingly teachable and discerning. And one of her best contributions to others is her ability to bring what she has learned right into their lives, to their benefit. Still, she's not a know-it-all, because she knows she *doesn't* know it all, and that a lifetime of learning and living won't even be sufficient time to learn it all.

She continues to learn how to balance the conflicting demands of her specific role as a woman. She recognizes that Iron Jane is not indestructible, but that she is only a weak vessel for God's powerful Spirit.

He teaches her all these things, often through other people.

FREE TO RISK AGAIN

Iron Jane may rightly consider herself weak when it comes to male-female relationships. She may have loved and lost more than once. But there's good news–the Bible reminds us that when we are weak, we are strong (2 Corinthians 12:10).

This means that she is learning where the chinks in her armor are, and instead of trying to trust in herself, she relies on the Lord to strengthen her. This keeps her from being frozen by the fear of failure. We know that even if we fall, God will be there to catch us.

Jane's safety net. My friend Juan Carlos Ortiz tells of making a spiritual discovery under the Big Top–at a circus. As he watched the highwire artists doing their amazing, death-defying stunts, he marveled at their bravery.

After the show he was able to talk to one trapeze artist. "How can you do these things so fearlessly?" he asked. "You do the same thing night after night, and yet you never seem afraid."

"Ah, no problema," commented one of the Latin American aerialists. "It's because of the net. We know the net is there. It will not only catch us if we fall, but it will help us to bounce back up. If we bounce back to the wire, many times the audience doesn't even know we've made a mistake; it looks like part of the act. Before the net was in place, we were so stiff and fearful that our performance wasn't half as good. Our secret is the net!"

And so is the secret of Iron Jane's success–the grace of God is the net. It is the blessed assurance that underneath us are the Everlasting Arms. The grace of God not only covers our sins, but he is so forgiving that if we fall, he will catch us and bounce us right back. If our hearts are his and we are daily putting on the armor of light, nothing can harm us—no failure, no mistake, not even sin. We don't have to be uptight about not being perfect—we can relax and enjoy a great performance.

DISCOVERING A NEW HEART

When Crystal received God's forgiveness for her sins, she had plenty of them to talk to him about. She had left her husband during a marital crisis. Once she was rid of him, she went out night after night, leaving her children alone, so she could visit singles bars. Before long she was leading a very promiscuous and wild life.

Crystal's sexual appetite and her low self-esteem were tangled up together. She became obsessed with men and her exploits with them. Even after her decision to trust God, her behavior didn't instantly change. Her church attendance was rare and she wasn't in a Bible study. However, little by little she found herself staying home with her children more often.

One night she called Pat, a Christian friend who had been praying for her. Her friend had pointed out the dangers of living such a sexually undisciplined life. Although she hadn't preached at Crystal judgmentally, she had let her know that her behavior wasn't exactly what God would choose for her.

Crystal told Pat, "You know, I went out with a man tonight. He's a guy I've known before, and he's a hunk. When he took me home, he assumed we were going to bed together, and he started coming on really strong."

Pat closed her eyes and quietly sighed. She had heard this story several times before–or so she thought. *Lord, won't she ever learn?* she thought to herself, feeling sad that Crystal kept selling herself so cheaply to men who were nothing but users. "So what happened?" Pat asked.

"Something I can't believe myself!" Crystal's voice was excited. "Pat, for the first time, I was turned off by his moves. I felt disgusted, and got out of the car before he could stop me."

"Did you run away from him because you felt guilty?"

"No! It wasn't guilt at all. I wasn't thinking about whether it was right or wrong. I just didn't want it. Something's changing inside of me, Pat. Somehow I feel stronger."

"I've been praying for you, Crystal. You're a beautiful woman and I know God wants to bless you with real love. It's just that you'll never find it as long as you're hanging out with that kind of man."

Crystal paused. "It's interesting you should say that. Last Sunday I went to mass. And just after I took communion, I was thinking about the guys I've been with, and that it's a really futile pattern of behavior I have. All of a sudden this thought hit me–'You deserve better.' I don't know where it came from, because I don't really think that about myself."

"I think it was the voice of God's Spirit, Crystal. Jesus bought you with his blood. You're his daughter now. You *do* deserve better, not because *you're* perfect but because he is, and you are his!"

> *True spirituality means allowing God to make us into the women he intended us to be.*

TRUE SPIRITUALITY

Crystal's story encourages me. I am reminded that God's strengthening grace is, in many ways, an inside job. Our sins may be as scarlet as Crystal's, or they may be more secret ones like hating, coveting, or being self-absorbed. The fact is, they are all sins, and they all separate us from God.

Our best efforts never quite bring us up to God's standards. Fortunately, he has an answer to that dilemma. He wants to bridge the gap for us, and he takes the initiative to do so.

True spirituality means allowing God to make us into the women he intended us to be. God wants us to commit ourselves to his Word and to realize that he has certain rules in place for our good.

But more than anything else, he longs to have our hearts given to him, so he is free to make them new. He changes us in quiet, unseen ways that no one really understands. The evidence is simply that we change. We become less absorbed with self-serving thoughts and actions. We become more like Jesus.

GIFTS AND PRIVILEGES

God has given us certain gifts and privileges that will help us grow into truly spiritual women:

Rebirth. First of all, like Whitney, we have to ask God to forgive us, and to give us his Spirit. We need to respond to God's invitation to follow him.

Scripture. God has provided his Word, the Bible, to give us guidance, counsel, and correction. We need to read it, remember what we read, and believe that God is speaking to us through it.

Prayer. God wants us to talk to him, and he wants to talk to us. In prayer, we establish a two-way relationship with our Creator, who will encourage us, listen to our requests, provide wisdom, and meet our needs.

Church. Gathering together in worship with other Christians is one of God's provisions for our spiritual health. Messages from his Word; sacraments like baptism and communion; group praise, worship and prayer all contribute to our inner strength.

Christian friends. God will bring Christian friends, pastors, teachers and counselors into our lives, especially if we ask him to do so. These caring individuals can help us find our way as spiritual women.

Spiritual gifts. God's Word describes special gifts that he gives his children—you can read about these in 1 Corinthians, chapters 12, 13 and 14. Ask to be filled with his Spirit. Best of all, ask another Christian to pray with you.

Positive attitude. We have a clear choice in our attitudes: we can be fretful and critical or we can be trustful and loving. It seems that an understanding of God's grace, mercy and love toward us doesn't leave much room for negative thinking. By choosing to live in gratitude and contentment, our spirits flourish. We remember every day that...

> ### *Gratitude is a form of worship.*

Forgiveness. You can read what Jesus had to say about forgiveness in Matthew 6:14. God's forgiveness toward us is blocked unless we forgive those who have wronged us. This is a vital step–and a daily step–toward spirituality.

Love. Jesus told us to keep his commandments, and then he said, "My commandment to you is this: Love each other as I have loved you" (John 15:12). Love undergirds all the gifts and commandments–God's own love poured into us and cleansing us inside, then extending out from us to other people.

WAR WITHOUT END, AMEN?

Much has been written about men and women, about women's issues, and about the conflicts that arise so frequently between the sexes. The longer we live, the more we realize that without God's help, we may be at war with the opposite sex for the rest of our lives. Our mutual grievances proliferate:

◆ Men misunderstand us; we misinterpret them.

◆ Men man-handle us; we manipulate them.

◆ Men control us through power; we control them through compliance and dependence.

◆ Men refuse to communicate with us; we refuse to stop nagging them.

◆ Men try to remain independent; women try to cling to them.

◆ Men feel victimized by their difficulties in the work-place; women feel victimized by men.

Is there any hope for healing? Only if we are willing to give up enough of ourselves to listen, learn and love. Only if we are prepared to accept the unchangeable, to change the unacceptable, and to have the wisdom to know the difference.

If we aren't willing or able to tackle such a fundamental biggie, we'll wind up agreeing with Katherine Hepburn's gloomy assessment: "Sometimes I wonder if men and women really suit each other. Perhaps they should live next door and just visit now and then."

Iron Jane emerges. Only Iron Jane can take on such a formidable task. She is prepared, because as she becomes the woman of God's design, she is able to truly love. And where there is love, there is understanding. There is delight. There is discovery. There is peace on the battlefield and celebration in the heart.

Chapter 10

Make Love, Not War

Men and women are differ-
ent in just about every way
imaginable. But why? In *Iron John*, Robert Bly searches for
answers in the symbolic imagery found in various pagan
myths. I think there's another story we ought to consider.

Some people categorize the biblical story of creation,
found in the book of Genesis, as a myth or a legend or a
fable. Others, including myself, believe that the Bible is
God's inspired Word, expressing our Father God's personality, plans, and principles.

In the Garden of Eden story, the Creator made a perfect paradise, and placed within it every kind of beautiful creature. Finally, and with great pleasure, he culminated his creation by making man out of the dust of the earth.

Once that first man had taken a good look at all the animals that graced the Garden, he began to recognize that they were all in pairs, but he was on his own. Since he was made in God's image, he had the capacity to feel emotions, unlike the animals and plants around him.

And he felt alone.

Adam's Maker wisely commented "It is not good for man to be alone." Therefore, in another sovereign creative act, God brought forth an exquisite mate for Adam. Eve was formed from her husband's rib, and was designed to fulfill him in every way.

> *The two first human beings were perfectly complementary; they brought absolute completion to each other.*

Then the snake entered the scene, pointing out the enticing fruit that hung on the Tree of the Knowledge of Good and Evil. Again we see that since the Creator had endowed these humans with his own kind of free will, they could make choices, either for better or for worse.

Once those two rebellious bites were taken, first by Eve and then by Adam, it wasn't only a conflict between good and evil that ensued. The battle of the sexes started when God confronted his foolish, wayward children.

Adam glared at Eve and said, "This is all your fault, you know."

Eve responded, "*My* fault? You ate the same thing I did, and I didn't force you, did I? It was the serpent's fault–you know that as well as I do. And don't think I didn't hear what you told God, either. When he asked you why you'd eaten it, you said, 'The woman you gave me–she gave it to me.' Why do *I* get blamed?"

"Frankly, Eve, it doesn't matter now anyway. We're cursed! You'd better start packing, because we're being evicted. We've eaten ourselves out of house and home, it seems."

The story goes on to say that woman would now have pain in childbirth, but would have children anyway because she would experience great desire for her husband, who would rule over her. The man, meanwhile, would sweat and struggle as he toiled in the fields trying to feed his family.

Dr. Larry Crabb writes,

God's judgment of Eve was on both her uniquely feminine capacity to give birth and her relationship with Adam. In other words, her physical attachment to Adam would lead to moments of excruciating pain (in childbirth) and her personal attachment would involve heartache and battle.

Adam's judgment was different; God required him to endure previously unknown difficulties as he sought to subdue his world. He would now have to work in a hostile environment where he would often fail, and to

live with a woman who would now be more concerned with her own needs than with his.[1]

THE SAME OLD STORY

Perhaps I cling to Bible stories with more dedication
than others, but this one isn't off base. Even skeptics have
to admit that this story rings true to modern experience.
How often have you seen the same old scenario played
out?

Wherever you look, you'll find women trying to understand why their men don't seem to be as concerned
about the couple's personal relationship as they themselves are. Men, in turn, get preoccupied with their work
and find themselves too tired to talk when they get home.

And when they do talk, the man can't understand why
the woman always wants to know if he still loves her.
After all, he said "I love you" at the wedding ceremony; as
far as he's concerned it's still true until he takes it back.

She takes ill-advised initiatives in an attempt to gain
what she wants. He blames her for problems he could
have prevented if he'd been paying attention.

She takes another bite, then he does, over and over.
When you think about it, man and woman both should
be screaming, "Help! I've fallen and I can't get up!"

Most of the researchers who have studied male-female
relationships never refer to the Garden of Eden tragedy.
Yet, interestingly, they base their teachings and techniques
on variations of the same archetypical premise:

> *A man's priorities are his function in the world and his independence. A woman's priorities are her relationships and her intimacy with her man.*

And as we have seen throughout this book, these sets of priorities don't automatically blend well.

SWORDS INTO PLOWSHARES

What does this have to do with Iron Jane? Iron Jane has faced combat and wants to talk peace. She wants to improve her relationships with men. She has come to the conclusion that minor compromises can be made without sacrificing who she is and without having hidden agendas.

If we are to be an Iron Jane, the kind of ceasefire we want begins with our own inner contentment. Much of this will happen as we become familiar with how and why men are so different from us, and with the realization that those differences aren't wrong.

"But what if Jake just doesn't *get* it?!" exclaimed Judy. "I mean, it takes all the fun out of it to have to explain everything a dozen times,... what I need, how I'm feeling. He'll just get that blank look on his face and ask, 'Well, what do you want me to *do?*' It's all so obvious to me; why doesn't he catch on?"

I smiled at her, hoping to offer as much encouragement as possible. "You've got a choice here," I replied. "Either you throw in the towel, scrap Jake, and chalk him up as another hopeless case you're glad you didn't get further involved with, *or* you get to work. If the relationship is worth anything to you, go get your Iron Jane armor..."

All of you Iron Janes out there, remember—your armor is not for the purpose of further combat with the men in your lives. It is the armor of light, the armor of God's Spirit. Reread Ephesians 6:13-17. Your armor includes key pieces called "salvation," "righteousness," "truth," "peace," "faith," and "the Word of God."

> *Perhaps if we begin to celebrate God's perfect design for men and women, we will find it possible to overcome the obstacles that weren't a part of the initial plan.*

It's unrealistic to think we can make our men more like us (sensitive and wonderful as we are) but it is realistic to develop the art of communication, accepting and even revelling in our differences, diligently working to establish a DMZ (demilitarized zone) with our name on it.

GOODBYE "IRON-DEFICIENCY ANEMIA"

So how does a Wounded Wendy or a Jaded Judy get to be an Iron Jane? To begin with, she strips off her outer suit of armor–that anti-male crust. By now she's come to see that it was only a protective covering for dealing with the slings and arrows of outrageous men. Such a tough exterior shielded her from all relationships, not just from the dangerous ones, and she has discovered that loneliness can be painful, too.

We become an Iron Jane through a process of spiritual re-armament. We arm ourselves with the trust that a Power greater than ourselves designed males and females to fit together in relationship. Our new knowledge and awareness energizes us and safeguards us against being unnecessarily vulnerable. We are stronger women because we are fortified with the power to discern why men act the way they do.

Their slings and arrows may penetrate from time to time, but the hurt is lessened because we've come to see that males are wired a certain way. It is our assignment to establish a basis for our "circuits" to operate in tandem, smoothly, without short-circuiting each other!

We Iron Janes never forget the importance of forgiveness, both giving it to others and receiving it from God. Iron Jane may be strong, but she remains sinful. I never called her "Teflon Jane," did I? We know we are fallible; we confess our nicks and scratches and sticky places as *sin* and we have more patience with the failings of others as a result.

We never forget our need for others, either. None of us can carry this off singlehandedly. We need like-minded friends. We need the Word of God and books based on its wisdom. We may need special help from professional counselors or from our pastor.

We are conscious of our new life every day. Taking our daily doses of iron into our minds and spirits not only cures our iron-deficiency anemia; it prevents its recurrence!

WHAT DOES SHE LOOK LIKE?

Iron Jane reclaims the word "feminine" and redefines it. Femininity is no longer characterized by a demure mademoiselle, dressed in lace, wobbling around on high heels, batting long eyelashes. Feminine, to Iron Jane, means a woman of the 90s, comfortable in the marketplace, respected by men who are intrigued with her solid-state strength. She is successful in her undertakings. She is motivated by love, not anger. She seeks peace, not power.

Iron Jane may be a single woman in her mid-twenties, just conquering her first "real" job. As she meets men and dates some of them, she sharpens her social skills. For her, dating isn't mostly self-oriented because she considers it a chance to meet and become friends with men, one of whom just might be Mr. Right.

By "Mr. Right," our model woman knows she doesn't mean "Mr. Perfect." She knows that both men and women fall short of the ideal. Furthermore, she realizes that men are not designed to be carbon copies of women. But she's willing to cooperate with the One who created us male and female to bring mutual understanding and peace into her interactions.

If and when Iron Jane becomes a wife, she's ready to

persevere in her pursuit of maturity and godliness. "Her children [if she has them] rise up and call her blessed; her husband also, and he praises her" (Proverbs 31:28).

She may be a lifelong stay-at-home housewife or she may be a careerwoman *par excellence*. More likely, she'll be something in-between, shifting her energies as the seasons of her life unfold.

It almost goes without saying that such a woman improves with age. The very life and love of God radiate from the center of her being as time goes on. She is able to share that life and love with her husband, her children, and her friends.

FAMILIARITY BREEDS CONTENTMENT

Armed with understanding and truth, Iron Jane is capable of being content in all circumstances. Let's review what makes it possible for her to see herself as a *counterpart* and not a *competitor*.

Physiologically, she knows that gender differences are much more than skin deep–more than glands and hormones. It's not just the male plumbing that is dissimilar to hers–*it's the entire blueprint*. Generally speaking, since men are predisposed to be more logical than emotional, more one-track than eight-track, Jane knows that this built-in contrast is meant to correspond with her alternative make-up.

Socially, Iron Jane recognizes that a man's primary focus is on *independence* rather than *intimacy*. Therefore, after a man has shared a time of intimacy with her, he'll probably snap back into his autonomous mode. A man's natural bent toward independence can feel like rejection, but Iron Jane has learned that it really isn't.

Emotionally, Iron Jane has learned to read her man's heart, not just his behavior. She doesn't cripple their relationship with unrealistic emotional expectations. She knows that a lot of men aren't as openly expressive as women, and therefore may feel a bit uncomfortable with women's tears. She also knows that doesn't mean something is wrong with them.

Needs and priorities are rarely the same for men and women, and Jane knows this well. She's willing to take inventory of herself, and then to let her man know what's important to her. She goes the extra mile in asking him to let her know what matters most to him, and then tries to meet his needs as he defines them. She doesn't project her own needs onto him, and then feel disappointed when he isn't satisfied.

Sexuality challenges Iron Jane to explore a secret part of her man's make-up–one he sometimes even hides from himself. She knows how important a man's sexuality is to his whole identity. Jane seeks to explore and enjoy her own sexuality and refuses to use sex as a weapon or a reward.

For her, sex is another way of communicating unconditional love and unity within a committed marriage relationship.

Communication is one of Iron Jane's most valuable tools–she cannot survive the battle of the sexes without it. She learns to control her "fight or flight" reflex, to speak the truth in love and to listen–very carefully. Jane knows that her man tends to share facts rather than feelings; her job is to let him know what she needs–in no uncertain terms.

And while it is typical for many men to quietly brood over problems in solitude, Iron Jane, like most women, prefers to verbalize her difficulties. She accepts this difference in communication style and she works within the givens of her situation.

Spirituality is Jane's secret weapon. Her most important "armor of light" is the protection of her soul and spirit. She keeps in touch daily with the Source of all strength and wisdom, who helps her to live her own life successfully and to spread love, peace, and harmony into other people's lives.

CEASEFIRE IN THE COLD WAR

Iron Jane is in close touch with her Creator, and respects his Master plan for males and females. The Original Designer never intended for men and women to be alike and he never planned for them to be combatants. His intention was for them to fit together perfectly, to delight one another, to find "completion" in each other.

But since Adam and Eve introduced sin into the picture, humankind has been in conflict, most elementally between husbands and wives.

Iron Jane has stopped being a smart woman making foolish choices in the battle of the sexes. She no longer chooses to declare war on men, neither does she raise the white flag of surrender. Jane knows that "the fear of man lays a snare," but that God's perfect love casts out fear.

She has strength because she has confidence. She has found inspiration to tackle the sometimes irritating differences between her and her man. And she has come to realize that the obstacles are there by design, to challenge her–and him–to be at their best. She finds genuine joy in the complementarity of her femaleness and his maleness.

Are you ready to join her? I hope you've gained the courage to tackle the irritating differences between "them" and "us." Perhaps, like me, you're ready to stop being "Cleopatra–the Queen of De-nial," or "Bitter Betty the Battle-Axe." Let's work together toward being Iron Jane, "the Princess of Peace."

NOTES

TWO
We're Wired So Differently!

1. Larry Crabb, *Men and Women; Enjoying the Difference* (Grand Rapids, Mich.: Zondervan, 1991), 133.

THREE
Two Different Worlds

1. Deborah Tannen, *You Just Don't Understand; Women and Men in Conversation* (New York: Ballantine, 1990), 47.
2. John Gray, *Men Are from Mars, Women Are from Venus: A Practical Guide for Improving Communication and Getting What You Want in Your Relationships* (New York: Harper-Collins, 1992), 95.
3. Gray, *Men Are from Mars, Women Are from Venus,* 105.
4. Barbara DeAngelis, *Secrets about Men Every Woman Should Know* (New York: Dell, 1990), 21.

FOUR
Is He Emotionally Brain Dead?

1. DeAngelis, *Secrets about Men Every Woman Should Know,* 147.
2. DeAngelis, *Secrets about Men Every Woman Should Know,* 153.
3. Tannen, *You Just Don't Understand,* 26.
4. Gray, *Men Are from Mars, Women Are from Venus,* 43.

FIVE
Who Needs What?

1. Crabb, *Men and Women*, 69.
2. Willard F. Harley, Jr., *His Needs, Her Needs: Building an Affair-proof Marriage* (Old Tappan, N.J.: Revell, 1986), 10.
3. Gray, *Men Are from Mars, Women Are from Venus*, 135-137.
4. James Dobson, *What Wives Wish Their Husbands Knew about Women* (Wheaton, Ill.: Tyndale, 1975), 82.
5. DeAngelis, *Secrets about Men Every Woman Should Know*, 30; 47-53.

SIX
First Things First

1. Crabb, *Men and Women*, 116.
2. David and Janet Congo, *The Power of Love; Overcoming the Love of Power in Your Relationships* (Chicago, Ill: Moody Press, 1993), 205.

SEVEN
What Are You Talking About?

1. Gary Smalley, *Hidden Keys to Loving Relationships* Seminar Supplement, 14.
2. Tannen, *You Just Don't Understand*, 75.
3. Gray, *Men Are from Mars, Woman Are from Venus*, 61.
4. Congo, *The Power of Love*, 84.

EIGHT
The Testosterone Syndrome

1. Dr. Archibald Hart, *The Sexual Man* (Waco, Tex.: Word Publishing, 1994).
2. Dobson, *What Wives Wish Their Husbands Knew about Women*, 115.

TEN
Make Love, Not War

1. Crabb, *Men and Women*, 142.

FOR FURTHER
READING

Much as been written about the so-called "battle of the sexes" by self-help writers, psychologists, researchers, and Christian counselors. It is good to be informed, and the books listed below may be helpful to you as you try to learn more about that very important relationship of yours.

Please don't assume, simply because a book appears on this list, that I'm wholeheartedly endorsing it. Some of these books come from a completely different philosophy than my own Christian perspective and may contain statements, subject matter or ideas that are provocative, sexually forthright, or entirely unacceptable to you. Nonetheless, I think these authors make some important points and provide perspectives that are worth consideration. Of course, others on the list are from the Christian point of view and offer additional spiritual insights as well as vital facts about men and women.

Choose whatever suits your situation, and enjoy reading!

Bly, Robert. *Iron John.* New York: Vintage Books, 1992.

Congo, David, and Janet. *The Power of Love; Overcoming the Love of Power in Your Relationships.* Chicago, Ill.: Moody Press, 1993.

Crabb, Larry. *Men and Women; Enjoying the Difference.* Grand Rapids, Mich.: Zondervan, 1991.

DeAngelis, Barbara. *Secrets about Men Every Woman Should Know.* New York: Dell, 1990.

Dobson, James. *What Wives Wish Their Husbands Knew about Women.* Wheaton, Ill.: Tyndale, 1975.

Gray, John. *Men Are from Mars, Women Are from Venus; A Practical Guide for Improving Communication and Getting What You Want in Your Relationships.* New York.: Harper-Collins, 1992.

Harley, Willard F., Jr. *His Needs, Her Needs, Building an Affair-proof Marriage.* Old Tappan, N.J.: Revell, 1986.

Hart, Archibald. *The Sexual Man.* Waco, Tex.: Word Publishing, 1994.

Mayhall, Jack and Carole. *Opposites Attach; Turning Your Differences into Opportunities.* Colorado Springs: Navpress, 1990.

Tannan, Deborah. *You Just Don't Understand; Women and Men in Conversation.* New York: Ballantine, 1990.

Lee Ezell
Ezell Communications
Box 7475
Newport Beach, CA 92658
(714) 251-1700